CLASSICBEER **7** STYLE**SERIES**

GERMAN WHEAT BEER

D0973885

ERIC WARNER

 A Brewers Publications Book

German Wheat Beer
By Eric Warner
Classic Beer Style Series
Edited by Tracy Loysen
Copyright 1992 by Eric Warner

ISBN 0-937381-34-9
Printed in the United States of America
10 9 8 7 6 5 4 3 2

Published by Brewers Publications,
a division of the Association of Brewers Inc.
PO Box 1679, Boulder, Colorado 80306-1679 USA
(303) 447-0816 • FAX (303) 447-2825

Direct all inquiries/orders to the above address.

Cover design by Robert L. Schram
Cover photography by Michael Lichter, Michael Lichter Photography
Cover art direction by Marilyn Cohen
Thanks to Rastal GmbH for donating the cover-photo glass.
Photo credits: pp. 6, 10, 18, 24, 53, 67, 68 from *Bayerns Bier-Burgen*
courtesy of Christian Sauer, Foto und Medienvertrieb; pp. 22 and 86
courtesy of Robert Liedl; p. 24 courtesy of Paulaner, North America;
pp. 12, 16, 57, 73, 82, 122 courtesy of G. Schneider & Sohn.

Table of Contents

Dedication

To Kristin, for your unconditional support of my passion and profession, and for being so understanding every time I make a mess of the kitchen and bathroom when I brew and bottle.

Acknowledgements

I would like to thank my good friend, Robert Liedl, for assisting me in the collection of data and illustrations for this book. When I returned home from Germany I had no idea I would be writing about my favorite beer style, and Rob was an invaluable link between Colorado and the wealth of information in Bavaria that I should have obtained before I left Germany.

Had Stephen Boss not been so patient in helping me locate the references Rob gave me, this book would only be half its size. Therefore, I extend my deepest gratitude to Steve Boss and the Coors Brewing Company for allowing me to use the Coors Technical Library in Golden, Colo.

Georg Schneider, Jr. provided me with much of the information on the history of German wheat beer, as well as many of the photographs and illustrations found in this book. Many thanks to him, his family and the Schneider & Sohn Weissbier Brewery in Bavaria for helping enrich this book and, more importantly, for being so dedicated to this classic beer style.

I would also like to extend my thanks to Jeff Coleman of the Paulaner Corporation of North America for providing me with information about the company he represents and the beer it produces, and for the photographs he contributed to the book.

Finally, I would like to thank Elizabeth Gold and Charlie Papazian of the Association of Brewers for allowing me to write this book. It was fun working with both of them on this project, and I think I can speak for all the brewers who read this when I say that without their commitment, the Classic Beer Style Series would not be as rich, informative and colorful as it is.

About the Author

Born and raised in Denver, Colo., Eric Warner successfully completed a degree in German Studies at Lewis and Clark College in Portland, Ore., before pursuing a formal education in Brewing Science in Germany. After three years of extensive brewery, lab and course work, Eric was awarded the degree 'Diplom-Braumeister' from the Technical University of Munich at Weihenstephan.

At home and in Europe Eric has worked in several breweries and visited scores of others. Most notably, he worked at Brauerei Widmann and Hofbrauhaus Moy, both in the Munich area, and at Denver's famed Wynkoop Brewing Co.

Eric is President of Blue River Brewing Consultants, working as an independent consultant to the microbrewing industry. He is also seriously considering starting his own microbrewery that would produce, among others beers, a German Style wheat beer. Eric's Weissbier was judged to be the best of the wheat beer category at the 1992 National Homebrew Competition. Eric lives in Lafayette, Colo., with his wife, Kristin, and canine companion, Supai. In his spare time he enjoys hiking, fly fishing, reading, tennis and, of course, homebrewing.

Preface

The world's beer culture is something each of us marvels at, and when the notion of world-class beer is mentioned, Germany instantly comes to mind. In contrast to Great Britain and Belgium, countries that have built their reputation on ales, Germany is popularly known as a country of lagers. Those who are familiar with the world's beers know that this is true, but they also know that for every rule there is an exception and in this case, the exception is a good one—wheat beer. The wheat beers of Germany are gaining in both popularity and availability in their own country and the rest of the world.

To say "the wheat beers of Germany" is much like saying the wines of France or the Scotch whiskies of Scotland; the wheat beers of Germany and Austria vary immensely in character, not only from region to region, but even within regions. It is both erroneous and misleading to randomly select one of these beers and say that it is exemplary of a German Weissbier. The scope of this book, however, does not allow for complete, detailed descriptions of the history, cultural significance, technological production parameters and analytical qualities of each substyle of German wheat beers. This book will focus primarily on pale Hefe Weissbier, the product that has emerged as the best selling and most widely consumed Weissbier in both Germany and the rest of the world. Other styles of German wheat beers, such as Kristall Weizen, Weizenbock and Berliner Weisse, will be outlined in Chapter 2, "Sensory Profile of German Wheat Beers." Recipes will be given for all of the primary styles of German wheat beers.

Introduction

The German word *Brotzeit*, literally translated, means bread time. So when the boss said "Brotzeit" at 9 a.m. on my first day of work in a small brewery outside of Munich, I thought it was time for a coffee break. I asked Lorenz where I could go to get some refreshments and he directed me to the small restaurant next door. I quickly located the only familiar faces in the room, those of the beer drivers I'd met earlier that morning. I sat down at their table and struggled to understand them as they babbled away in the local Bavarian dialect. I was able to understand the waitress when she came and asked what we wanted. I was the first to order at our table, and sheepishly blurted out the word "Kaffee."

Suddenly I felt like I was in one of those commercials for financial advisers, where the room suddenly goes totally silent. Then the youngest beer driver looked at me, and began talking to me while shaking his head. I couldn't understand a word he said, but it seemed clear he was chastising me. The oldest driver just stared down his swollen red nose at me in sheer disbelief. Finally Rudi, who reminded me of Barney Rubble, told the waitress to bring us four Weissbiers, and before I could open my mouth to explain how I was a good boy and wouldn't dare drink before noon, let alone while on the job, Wilma (that really was her name) was headed to the refrigerator.

This wasn't my first Weissbier, and after we had said "Prost" and taken our first sip, I looked around the room and noticed that we weren't the only ones who were enjoying the frothy, full-bodied wheat beer produced at the brewery right next door. This was a working man's pub, and at that moment I realized that this was the beer of choice in the German state that boasts one of the highest per capita beer consumption levels in the world. I had seen plenty of students and club goers enjoying this turbid brew, but on September 21, 1987, I became a reborn Weissbier drinker.

The first Weissbier I had ever drunk tasted awful to me. I was in Munich for a junior-year-abroad program, and Bruce, one of the guys in our group, said he had tried this new beer that all the Germans on his floor were drinking. Eager to try anything at the age of 20 (especially because I was legal there), I quickly hurried over to the student restaurant in Bruce's dorm building to try a Weissbier. I was disappointed as soon as I saw it. My beer appreciation skills had not yet developed enough for me to grasp the concept of unfiltered or bottle-conditioned beers, and a clear, dark lager beer represented to me the pinnacle of the brewer's craft. This milky-colored beer with its floating chunks of yeast was suspect before I even tasted it. And when I did, I looked at Bruce, shook my head and told him this was one of the worst beers I had ever tasted. I wrote off Weissbier from that day on. Or so I thought.

Over the course of the next few months, Bruce and many of my German friends urged me to try the turbid brew again and again. Gradually its cloudiness ceased to offend me, and slowly I began to develop an appreciation for the complex taste of Hefe Weissbier. Just as I had progressed to the point where I would actually buy and drink an entire Weissbier, it was time to return home to the land of pale, bland lagers. I had only been back in America for a few weeks when I realized I was missing out on something, and I decided to return to Germany after graduation to pursue an education in brewing.

On that fateful day when I began my formal training as a brewer, I realized just how coveted Hefe Weissbier is in the area around Munich. If the Germans were having it on their "coffee break," then it must be pretty good stuff. Indeed, that beer was as fine a Weissbier as they come, but what really made it taste so good wasn't the rich, spicy palate of the beer, or its bubbly, refreshing and thirst-quenching taste, but the fact that my co-workers had invited me to drink it with them. My co-workers were showing me, a stranger in a foreign land, how to fit in. Beer always tastes better in the company of others, and on my first day of work in that small village brewery where I couldn't understand a word anyone was saying, that Weissbier tasted pretty good.

TERMINOLOGY

Before going any further, it would be wise to set the record straight about all of those big German words that begin with W and have something to do with wheat beer.

Weizen. A German word that literally means wheat, but colloquially means wheat beer or Weissbier, particularly in Swabia.

Weissbier. Weiss means white, but anyone who has ever drunk a Weissbier knows that its color is more golden yellow, not white. But Weissbier is much paler than the dark beers that were so popular in Bavaria in earlier times, so the word white is used relatively.

Hefe Weissbier or *Hefe Weizen.* These terms refer to

any Weissbier that has yeast (Hefe) in it; i.e., a bottle-conditioned Weissbier.

Kristall Weizen. A term used to describe any filtered wheat beer. Kristall Weizen is more popular in Austria than in Germany.

Berliner Weisse. By German law, beer brewed in this style can only be labeled Berliner Weisse if it has been brewed in Berlin. It is made, as are all Weissbiers, with a certain percentage of wheat malt. Berliner Weisse has a much lower starting gravity, is hopped less, and has a decidedly more lactic character than southern Weissbier. Phenolic character is not present in a Berliner Weisse.

Dunkles Weissbier. Dunkles Weissbier is most commonly found in Bavaria. Literally, the words mean dark white beer, a contradiction in terms. It is made with dark barley or wheat malts. The color is further deepened with colored malts or colored beer (derived from beer that has been made with a higher than normal percentage of black malt). Dunkles Weissbier is similar in flavor to Hefe Weissbier, but its rich, malty aroma is more pronounced than the aroma of a pale Weissbier.

Weizenbock. A wheat beer that is brewed to bock strength (at least 16 °Plato). It is usually dark, but pale versions are also found. Many breweries brew a Weizenbock as a Christmas beer.

Leichtes Weissbier. Leicht means light; believe it or not, light Weissbiers are selling well in Germany. The main characteristics of a Leichtes Weissbier are similar to those of a full-strength Weissbier, but the overall impression is diluted.

1

Why the Elixir of Life is so Popular

Weissbier currently is one of Germany's most popular beer styles, but this has not always been the case. Though it enjoyed immense popularity during the 17th and 18th centuries, in the 19th century it was on the verge of extinction. It might have gone that route had it not been saved from the jaws of death by a brewer with vision, Georg Schneider. Still, Weissbier sales fell to an all-time low in 1951, with production figures barely topping 100,000 hL. At the time this amount was little more than 1 percent of the beer produced in Bavaria.[1] Now, though, Weissbier is back stronger than ever. Today it accounts for 22 percent of the beer produced in Bavaria,[2] which translates to 6.3 million hL, and it is the best seller for many breweries that produce a variety of other beers. Some breweries that produce only Weissbier report sales that approach 1 million barrels per year. Weissbier breweries are working feverishly to keep pace with the demand for this unique beer style.

Weissbier is popular not only in Germany, but in other European countries as well. In countries outside of Europe Weissbier sales are also booming. A number of United States breweries are making their own interpretations of Weissbier,

Industrial gothic at the Kaltenberg Brewery. Jesuits served beer here as early as the 18th century. Today, like many other Bavarian "Castle-breweries," Kaltenberg brews beer for commercial purposes.

and American wheat beer is now a recognized style in the United States.

To what can we attribute this incredible renaissance? Perhaps the best way to ascertain the secrets of Weissbier's success in the last few decades would be to ask the consumers themselves why they prefer to drink it over other types of German beers. A consumer poll entitled "44 user's reasons for Weissbier consumption"[3] did exactly this. The following top 11 list (10 just wasn't enough) is excerpted here:

11) "Earlier I always had problems with my stomach and digestion. In the clinic I was advised to begin carefully with Weissbier after my gall operation. For several years now Weissbier has been my elixir of life."

10) "We started a soccer club called 'Weizen' here in Riesgau several years ago. This isn't a sport club, rather a social club that has dedicated itself to Weissbier. The Weissbier drinkers in our group are always becoming more numerous."

9) "Weissbier with a bit of yeast is simply chic, healthy and easy to digest. Every 14 days we have our ladies' Weissbier gathering."

8) "Up until a few years ago we bowlers drank pils or normal keg beer almost exclusively; now most drink Weissbier. The consumption level of beer has become less, and the number of schnapses has been reduced considerably."

7) "Earlier my wife never drank Weissbier, but in the meantime her friends have corrupted her with it. We've even purchased Weissbier schooners to be used with drinking straws because of it."

6) "If we drink 2 pints of Export in the morning, we're tired; with Weissbier in the same quantity this isn't so."

5) "When I was 15 I had a lot of zits. Our doctor prescribed me pills, and every evening I was supposed to drink a pint of Weissbier, but not more. Within a few weeks the zits had disappeared. That came from the nicotinic acid in the beer yeast, maintained the doctor. Since then my friends and I are true Weissbier fans and are familiar with over 50 brands of Weissbier."

4) "Mornings, and particularly after church on Sunday, the 'Weisse' tastes best to me."

3) "Recently a women's magazine wrote that Weissbier yeast is even supposed to help with hemorrhoids."

2) "The nicest thing about Weissbier are the burps, which also bring the bad air out of the stomach."

And the number one reason why Weiss is nice....

1) "After a real beer evening (i.e. session) with Pils, or now in the spring season with double bock, only Weissbier still tastes good the morning after."

It is pretty easy to expose three main drives behind the Weissbier craze from our top 11 list: Weissbier is healthy, it's in and, most importantly, it tastes great.

Hefe Weissbier is a popular drink in Germany because

of the intrinsic nutritional value of the yeast. Doctors and women's magazines have long heralded the benefits of Weissbier for the human body, particularly the skin. Yeast contains a variety of vitamins, trace mineral elements and protein compounds that are essential to the human body, and the recommended daily allowance of many of these substances can be met by consuming just one pint of Weissbier per day.[4] The wealth of vitamin B complexes in yeast accounts for its great physiological value not only for humans, but for livestock as well. The unlucky yeast cells that do not make it into a bottle of Hefe Weissbier or into a new fermentation are often used by the pharmeceutical or feed industries. Too much yeast (more than 30 grams per day) may produce increased levels of uric acid in the blood, which can lead to gout. Humans should not consume more than two grams of nucleic acid per day, which corresponds to 30 grams of yeast.[5] Weissbier has approximately four grams of yeast per liter, which means that those who drink more than seven liters of the frothy brew per day may be jeopardizing their health (in more ways than one!).

One of the less tangible reasons for the increased popularity of Weissbier in the last few decades has to be its appeal as a chic, or "in" beer to drink. This phenomenon is perplexing because the breweries that make other products in addition to Weissbier do not necessarily market the Weissbier more intensely. Southern Germany's breweries tend to refrain from using sleek models or rock stars to advertise their Weissbiers, yet sales are strong enough to make the marketing director of any large North American brewery drool. The overwhelming majority of small breweries have an extremely local market and do virtually no advertising. The Weissbier renaissance is truly a grass roots movement, unlike the light beer revolution in the United States that has been fueled by the high-powered, well-financed advertising of the breweries promoting such products.

Weissbier is not only hip in the bars and nightclubs of Southern Germany, but is gaining popularity in northern cities like Cologne, Berlin and Hamburg as well. There is no doubt that Pilsener is still king in Northern Germany and will be for quite some time, but Northern Germans are buying more and more Weissbier all the time, both at home and on their vacations to Southern Germany. Weissbier is appealing to the Northern Germans not only because of the intrinsic qualities of the beer, but also because it represents something exotic. Northern Germans have a peculiar love/ hate relationship with Bavaria. In a way, it is similar to the relationship the 49 United States of America have with Texas. Bavaria is a fascinating and beautiful place that offers plenty of opportunities for outdoor activities. It still officially labels itself "The Free State of Bavaria," although it has been incorporated into the Federal Republic of Germany for quite some time. It is a place where, according to the Northern Germans, the people think slowly and talk funny. The turbid Weissbier, served in half-liter glasses, is a specialty of the South. In the North it is next to impossible to find a brewery that produces unfiltered beer, and the standard glass size is a third of a liter.

In the South itself Weissbier occupies a peculiar position. It seems to be a beer that most people either die for or can't stand, though some alternate between binging on Weissbier for awhile and drinking lager for a couple of months. In Bavaria, Helles is really the mainstay beer, probably because it has a more neutral taste and is less expensive than Pils or Weissbier. At construction sites the workers can be observed quaffing bottles of cheap Helles. When out for a night on the town, though, people often splurge on a more exotic beer, and many nightclubs serve only Weissbier or Pils, asking three times the price that would be paid for these beers in a restaurant.

Weissbier has not been able to break into the *Volksfest* (people's fair) circuit of outdoor festivals that begin in late spring and end in early fall. The most notable of these gatherings is the Oktoberfest, at which some eight million liters of beer are served in 16 days. Only an infinitesimal fraction of this amount is Weissbier; even religious Weissbier drinkers imbibe the lager beer to avoid friction. Asking for a Weissbier at many of these fests is a bit like asking a waitress to add hot water to the decaf coffee you just ordered; she may serve it to you, but she probably won't be too friendly for the rest of the night.

Weissbier does have its special moments when it is spotlighted and showcased in all its glory. Weissbier is the

A typical Bavarian pub, or Bräustüberl.

"breakfast beer" of Southern Germany. In Bavaria it often rounds out a trio that includes *Weisswurst* and *Brezen*. Weisswurst, or "white sausage," is made of veal and seasoned with parsley. It has a delicate flavor and traditionally is served with a sweet mustard. Brezen is the German word for pretzel. The Brezen served with Weissbier and Weisswurst are soft and about as big around as a pancake. The classic Weisswurst breakfast is always served before noon, and it is quite popular on weekends. It is the Brunch of Bavaria.

This breakfast ritual comes to a crescendo during *Fasching* (Carnival) in Bavaria. Revelers drink Champagne or lager beer through the night at a Fasching party (or ball, as these gatherings are often called), but in the wee hours or next morning it is customary to have the classic Weisswurst breakfast. Fasching seems to be one time of year when Weissbier flourishes. Although this celebration officially begins on the 11th of November every year, it doesn't really get going until after January 6, and it comes to a wild climax during the weekend prior to Ash Wednesday. On this weekend the cities and villages in Weissbier country erupt with a bacchanalian festiveness that is topped only by the simultaneous celebrations in Rio, Cologne, Venice and New Orleans.

Regardless of the time of year, Weissbier enjoys a strong following on a day-to-day basis. In the pubs and restaurants of Southern Germany, one can always order a Weissbier. Weissbier is arguably the pride of Bavaria, more so than even the Bavarian Helles style of beer, which has been imitated in Germany and in the rest of the world to a much greater extent than Weissbier. Many red-blooded Bavarians pledge allegiance to Weissbier as a way of affirming their loyalty to their state.

For most Weissbier drinkers, the allure of this beer is not the vitamin content of the Hefe Weissbier, nor its

In the last century, as no one wanted to know anything more about wheat beer brewing, the brewery founder Georg Schneider bet on his knowledge and experience and began to brew "Schneider Weisse" in the Weissen Bräuhaus in Munich according to his own recipe. This pioneering spirit saved the old Bavarian Hefeweissbier from being forgotten.

stature as the most popular drink in the local night club or pub, but simply its unique taste. I can't count the number of Germans I know who drink no other kind of beer. Forget the malty, breadlike Munich dark, or the crisp, refreshing well hopped Pils, insist many. They do not realize that most educated beer drinkers would kill for a chance to sample these other classic beer styles of Southern Germany. To them no other beer satisfies like a Weissbier.

THE HISTORY OF WHEAT BEER BREWING IN BAVARIA

As one of the first grasses to be cultivated by man, wheat is not a surprising ingredient in some of the world's first beers. The Babylonians used wheat in their primitive brews and, according to Martin Hürlimann, beer historian and owner of Brauerei Hürlimann in Zurich, Switzerland, the Babylonians were making a lot of wheat beer in the 400 years prior to their demise. Hopefully this is not an evil omen for the Bavarians!

How the early Germanic tribes made beer is not certain, but it is known that at the end of the Middle Ages both barley and wheat were being used, and all the beer was top fermented. The first Weissbiers (so labeled because they were noticeably paler than the other beers of the day, which were brown) were probably produced in the latter half of the 15th century by the Degenbergers. This noble clan awarded itself the privilege of brewing Weissbier in the Bavarian Forest area and in Bohemia, and built the first known Weissbier brewery in the town of Schwarzach. Duke Wilhelm IV extended the Degenbergers' authority to brew Weissbier to an even larger area, but later Duke Albrecht V demanded that they pay a surcharge on the Weissbier they were selling. When the Baron Hans Sigmund of Degenberg refused to pay, maintaining that doing so would contradict the freedoms of the Degenbergers, tempers escalated and a feud arose.

The resolution of this conflict was quite simple. Old Hans Sigmund had spent too much time arguing and making beer and had failed to procreate. His lineage ended with his death in 1602, and his rights to brew became the property of the Bavarian house of Dukes and the Wittelsbacher empire. Duke (and later prince) Maximilian I was a clever businessman, and immediately investigated the possibilities of becoming a brewery operator. He had someone familiarize him with the brewing process and had the Schwarzach brewery appraised. Apparently he was impressed with what he saw, because shortly thereafter he declared that the brewing of Weissbier was an exclusive right of the house of Dukes, and he placed a ban on public Weissbier brewing. Maximilian's next step was to bring the braumeister at Schwarzach to Munich to oversee construction of a Weissbier brewery next to the brownbier brewery there. (It is not unlikely that some of us have visited the site of Munich's first Weissbier brewery; today the Hofbrauhaus Munich is located there.) Many of the other breweries the Degenbergers had built were incorporated into the royal network of Weissbier breweries, and the brewery in Schwarzach was renovated from 1687 to 1689. A visit paid to Schwarzach today is well worth the effort; the building has been well preserved since these 17th century renovations.

Following Maximilian's takeover of the Degenberger breweries, the demand for Weissbier began to increase dramatically. The noble and elite in Bavaria enjoyed its effervescent qualities. Compared to the brownbier, it was much more refreshing and spritzy. Because the more refined were drinking this new beverage, those on the lower rungs of the social ladder also wanted to drink Weissbier. Call it an early form of keeping up with the Schmidts, but the common folk figured that if this beer was good enough for royalty and nobility, then it was OK for them, too. If this was not enough to keep the Weissbier flowing, the governing body of the house of Dukes ordered that all publicans who were serving brownbier also had to obtain ducal Weissbier, lest the right to operate the pub be revoked!

The Weissbier breweries during the 17th and 18th centuries were bursting at the seams as the brewers struggled to keep pace with the public's demand for the ducal drink. Though the Weissbier brewery in Munich was just minutes away from several churches in the center of town, the brewers there could not find the time to attend even the shortest of masses. In the early 18th century a small chapel was built within the walls of the brewery. The brew knaves scratched together enough money to procure an altar and altar painting, and a priest held services for them in the brewery! The revenue generated by the sales of Maximilian's beloved brew was so great that he was able to finance part of his costs in the Thirty Years' War from Weissbier proceeds.

Another testament to the popularity of Weissbier at the time is the story of the *Bierstrasse* (beer street). Apparently the students in the town of Ingolstadt (located about 60 miles north of Munich) were so captivated by Weissbier that shipments from the ducal brewery in Kelheim could not keep pace with their thirst. Part of the problem was that the beer had to be shipped more than 25 miles upriver from Kelheim along the Danube, a method of transportation that was far too time consuming. To satiate the desires of the students, a special road, appropriately named the Bierstrasse, was built through the hilly countryside from Kelheim to Ingolstadt to provide the pubs with Weissbier more expediently.

Slowly, however, the demand for Weissbier waned. Once it entirely permeated the beer market, this once noble drink of the gentry became as common as water and its novelty was lost. At the same time, the monastic breweries in Bavaria had refined their brewing process, and the brownbier tasted better than ever. By the end of the 18th century Weissbier sales had slacked off to the point of unprofitability, and the reign of ducal brewing was over. One by one, the breweries of Maximilian's empire were sold off, including the ones in Schwarzach and Munich. In 1802 the Weissbier brewery in Munich was leased to someone in the private sector, and as output decreased many of the rooms in the brewery became vacant. In 1808 the adjacent royal brownbier brewery took over the empty rooms of Maximilian's showcase Weissbier brewery.

Were it not for the foresight of brewer Georg Schneider, Weissbier would probably just be another entry under the heading of "extinct beers" in the annals of brewing history. In the brewing year of 1855-56 the lease on the "Weisses Brauhaus" in Munich came up and Schneider became the new tenant. Sales of his Weissbier were not exactly boom-

The old G. Schneider & Sohn Brewery in Munich in 1891.

ing, but he was planning for the future by attempting to privatize the rights to brew Weissbier. Schneider knew that the brownbier brewery needed the adjacent space in the Weissbier brewery. After lengthy negotiations, he played his trump card and said he would vacate the Weissbier brewery if the rights to brew Weissbier were handed over to him and the public. He was successful, and in 1872 the 250-year reign of royal brewing came to an end. In the same year, Schneider purchased the old Maderbräu brewery in downtown Munich, and within the seven years from 1874 to 1881, the malt usage of the brewery tripled. Slowly Weissbier made a comeback, and Weissbier breweries began to crop up all over Bavaria, as well as in Swabia and parts of Austria.

Despite the renewed popularity of Weissbier, it did not regain the huge following it had had in the days of the Degenbergers and Maximilian. Blame the Czechs for this perhaps; lagers, and in particular the new wunderkind

Pilsener, were revolutionizing the European beer market. Weissbier had once been the drink of kings and queens, but lager beers were the new chic beers at the end of the 19th century. Weissbier managed to persevere, and many breweries survived by brewing lagers in addition to Weissbier, but it was not until well after World War II that the real Weissbier renaissance began.

Today there are some 200 breweries producing Weissbier in Bavaria, Baden-Württemberg and Austria. Even breweries in Switzerland and other German states produce Weissbiers. Many of the smaller Weissbier breweries in Bavaria enjoy almost a cult following. These are breweries that do virtually no advertising, yet their Weissbier sales are booming. Loyalty to these breweries is partly responsible for this phenomenon, but another factor is that people like what they are used to. Because the Weissbier in one village tastes quite different from that of the next, it can be a great shock to the palate to try a Weissbier from the brewery down the road. Germans are some of the biggest armchair brewmasters on the face of the earth, and although some are objective in their criticism of other beers, to many the best beer around is either the one they have been drinking for the last 20 years, or the beer that is brewed locally. Often it's the same beer.

There is a vast number of small "farmer" breweries, as they are often called, trying to survive on the loyalty of the local market, competing against the large Munich breweries and other giants in Bavaria. The individuality of these Weissbiers, coupled with a bit of product inconsistency, makes them so special that a pilgrimage to Bavaria is necessary in order to appreciate them. You will not find these Weissbiers in the import section of even the largest North American liquor stores. Book your flight now, because the large breweries that produce Weissbier are out-muscling the smaller

Even today Weissbier is still delivered in Mercedes trucks, just as it was 60 years ago.

breweries with competitive pricing. The Weissbiers from many of the large breweries are exceptional, but there has been an increased tendency toward homogeneity among them as competition in the German beer market has stiffened. More and more beers are being sold in supermarkets in Germany, and it is usually the mass-produced Weissbiers that are retailed in these outlets.

The future for Weissbier looks quite bright at this time. Sales of Weissbier are at an all-time high, and now that the two Germanies have been reunited, the well-established breweries in the West have been able to increase their sales in the East. In 1990, Bavarian breweries experienced a 14 percent increase in production over 1989, and during the second half of 1990 the production in the breweries of the old GDR declined more than 50 percent.[6] Wheat beers now account for 22 percent of the Bavarian market. Only Bavarian Helles can claim greater sales than Weissbier, with a market share of 28 percent. Many breweries have begun production of light Weissbiers, which promise to sell well as light beers steal an ever greater percentage of the German beer market. More than one brewery has now even begun producing an alcohol-free Weissbier! Although many small, country breweries are being forced to close, Germany is experiencing a brewpub trend similar to that of other beer drinking countries. Many of these brewpubs are serving Weissbier, and other small breweries are being saved by their Weissbiers.

Weissbier was virtually unheard of in North America 10 years ago, but now there are at least a dozen German Weissbiers available in the United States. Jeff Coleman, head of the Paulaner North America Corporation, says the sales of Paulaner's Hefe Weizen are booming. He notes that sales of this beer were last among Paulaner's labels in the United States five years ago, but now the Oktoberfest and the Weissbier are neck and neck for the lead, with the other four Paulaner products trailing behind. The strongest markets for Weissbier in the United States are in the Midwest, particularly the areas in and around Chicago, Milwaukee and Minneapolis. Weissbier accounts for 65 percent of Paulaner's sales in the Midwest. The Hefe Weizen is also doing well in newer markets. Weissbier is a popular choice among American microbrewers, and many small breweries in the United States produce their interpretation of Weissbier as their flagship product. The number one selling microbrewed beer in Australia, Red Back, is also a Weissbier.

Having been saved from impending doom, Weissbier is back stronger than ever, and for at least the next couple of decades, sales of this beer should continue to rise. Aside from its extraordinary, unique taste and its nutritional appeal, Hefe Weissbier is also a chic beverage at the moment. Its turbid appearance and special glass set it apart from the mainstream lagers. Whether one is in a pub nestled in the Bavarian countryside, a hot nightclub in Berlin, a ski resort in Austria, a brewpub in the United States, or a café in Sydney, one thing is clear: Weiss is nice!

2

Sensory Profile of German Wheat Beers

There are many variations among the different styles of Weissbier in Germany. The pale Hefe Weissbier is the most popular on the whole, but some of the other German wheat beers have a rich tradition and enjoy a loyal following. With the exception of Berliner Weisse and isolated beer styles similar to it, the Weissbiers of Southern Germany have three common characteristics in addition to the fact that they all contain wheat. First, Weissbiers are highly carbonated. In fact, they contain 1 1/2 to 2 1/2 times the amount of CO_2 that American and German lagers do. Second, true Weissbiers are very lightly hopped. Bitterness should not exceed 18 IBU if the beer is to be true to style. Finally, they have a very typical phenolic and estery-fruity aroma and flavor that sets them apart from any other beer. This character is attributable to many fermentation parameters, but the yeast strain is the most important.

An in-depth discussion of the characteristics and chemical composition of pale Hefe Weissbier is presented in Chapter 4, but for now, let's take a look at the sensory profiles of the different German wheat beers, as well as the ingredients and brewing methods that give each its own, distinctive character.

A look down Main Street in Freising, Germany. This small town north of Munich is home to the brewing school at Weihenstephan as well as two breweries that produce Weissbier.

- Pale Hefe Weissbier -

Original Gravity: 1.047-1.056 (11.5-13.8 °Plato)
Apparent Final Gravity: 1.015-1.020 (3.7-4.9 °Plato)

Apparent Degree of Attenuation: 80-86%
Real Degree of Attenuation: 65-70%
pH: 4.0-4.5
Bitterness: 10-18 IBU
Color: 3.5-9.5 SRM (8-24 EBC units)
Alcohol Content: 4.0-4.5% w/v; 5.0-5.6% v/v
Calories per 12 oz. Serving: 151-178 (425-500 kcal/1,000 g)

If you walk into a pub in Bavaria and say "Ein Weissbier, Bitte," nine times out of 10, the beer you get will have the characteristics listed above. Weissbier is perhaps a bit stronger than an American or German lager, but its starting gravity falls into the category of Vollbier, or "fullbier," which is the class of standard gravity beers in Germany. The alcoholic strength of Weissbier is reflected in its high degree of attenuation, yet the starting gravity of a Weissbier is high enough that it cannot be labeled thin. The high levels of carbonation and attenuation make the beer refreshing and very drinkable, while the high starting gravity and high protein content give it some body. The combination makes for an ideal session beer to many Germans.

The pH of a Weissbier is fairly standard for top-fermented beers. The color of a pale Weissbier is light to ruddy-orange. With the exception of light Weissbier and Berliner Weisse, German wheat beers are not for calorie counters.

The trademark of a Hefe Weissbier is its phenolic, estery flavor and aroma. This is one style of beer where a phenolic note is desirable and a fruity nose is expected. Since hopping rates are low, these characteristics come to the fore, along with a slight maltiness. An in-depth discussion of the flavor and aroma of pale Hefe Weissbier can be found in Chapter 3, "Physical and Chemical Composition." Brewing procedures are outlined in detail in Chapter 4.

- Dunkles Weissbier -

Original Gravity: 1047-1055 (11.5-13.5 °Plato)
Apparent Final Gravity: 1016-1018 (4.0-4.4 °Plato)
Apparent Degree of Attenuation: 78-84%
Real Degree of Attenuation: 63-68%
pH: 4.15-4.55
Bitterness: 10-16 IBU
Color: 10-23 SRM units (25-60 EBC units)
Alcohol Content: 3.8-4.4% w/v; 4.8-5.5% v/v
Calories per 12 oz. Serving: 150-166 (423-468 kcal/1,000 g)

Very popular in the regions of lower Bavaria and the Bavarian forest, Dunkles Weissbier displays many of the same characteristics as the pale Weissbier, but with a more pronounced malty aroma and flavor. The phenolic impression is still present, as is the estery or fruity note, but the dark malt masks some of these flavors that are near the threshhold level of perception. The starting gravities of Dunkel Weizen are in the same range as pale Weizen, but the alcohol

A Bavarian farmer is picking up spent grains for his cows at a local brewery.

content may be slightly less (there is less fermentable extract in dark malt). The CO_2 content is also similar. The color of Dunkles Weissbier ranges from 10 to 23 SRM units (25 to 60 EBC units). Dark Weissbiers are made using dark barley or wheat malts, dark cara malts, color malts or colored beer. Often combinations of these are employed to allow for adjustments in the quality of the different malt types. Medium-hard to hard water can be used for brewing Dunkles Weissbier without jeopardizing the flavor of the finished beer. A classic dark Weissbier should have a malty, breadlike aroma and flavor; to maximize this characteristic, a double decoction mash is commonly used. The rest times and temperatures are very similar to those for the pale Weissbier double decoction mash, but boiling times for the decoction mashes are longer, up to 45 minutes. Protein rests may also have to be longer than those for a pale Weissbier, as the dark malts contain less free amino nitrogen than pale malts. The rest of the process steps are similar to those for a pale Weissbier.

- Weizenbock -

Original Gravity: 1065-1080 (16-20 °Plato)
Apparent Final Gravity: 1026-1032(6.5-8.0 °Plato)
Apparent Degree of Attenuation: 75-80%
Real Degree of Attenuation: 61-65%
pH: 4.1-4.3
Bitterness: 12-18 IBU
Color: 10-29 SRM units (25-75 EBC units)
Alcohol Content: 5.6-6.5% w/v; 7.0-8.1% v/v
Calories per 12 oz. Serving: 213-266 (600-750 kcal/1,000 g)

In 1907, in the midst of heated discussion about whether or not a brewery should use religious words to name their secular products, a new beer appeared the market that bore the name of a person of religious significance—Aventinus. St. Aventinus was a Bishop on the seventh hill in Rome. Munich residents at the time insisted that the Schneider and Sons Brewery named its beer after Aventinstrasse, the street into which the brewery had expanded. In fact, the beer was named after an historian by the name of Aventinus, who came to fame in Bavaria in the 16th century.

In any case, anyone who has ever drunk a Weizenbock is well aware of the spiritual mood such a beer can induce. To be worthy of the designation Weizenbock, a beer must be brewed to at least 1.066 (16 °Plato) starting gravity. Aventinus, which is arguably the first Weizen beer to be intentionally marketed as a Weizenbock, weighs in at a hefty 1.075 (18.5 °Plato). Many breweries produce a wheat bock as a Christmas beer, and they are quite popular during the Lenten season as well.

Naturally, Weizenbocks are high in alcohol, and some are more liberally hopped than the lighter Weissbiers. The phenolic character of a Weizenbock is usually overpowered by the aroma of the alcohols, the malty sweetness imparted by the higher gravity and the use of dark malts, and the increased fruity character of the bouquet, which is attributable to the higher ester content of these beers. Wheat bocks of Southern Germany are usually dark in color. This color may be created by the use of dark or chocolate malts, or colored beer, though some are brewed using only pale malts. The color is intensified by employing a decoction mash. Boiling times for the decoction mashes are 30 to 45 minutes. Fermentation and conditioning times are longer than those for pale Weissbier due to the increased strength of the wort, and pitching rates are increased to compensate for reduced yeast reproduction. To combat the increased ester content of the beer and to help speed the fermentation process, the levels of air or oxygen dissolved into the wort prior to fermentation are often increased.[7]

- Kristall Weizen -

Original Gravity: 1.045-1.055 (11.0-13.5 °Plato)
Apparent Final Gravity: 1.016-1.020 (4.0-4.9 °Plato)
Apparent Degree of Attenuation: 76-85%
Real Degree of Attenuation: 62-69%
pH: 4.1-4.4
Bitterness: 10.5-18.5 IBU
Color: 3.5-5.0 SRM units (8-12 EBC units)
Alcohol Content: 5.1-5.5% v/v ; 4.1-4.4% w/v
Calories per 12 oz. Serving: 158-170 (444-478 kcal/1,000 g)

Appropriately named for its brilliantly clear appearance, this is the only German Weissbier that is completely devoid of yeast once it is packaged. However, because the process steps and ingredients used to brew a Kristall Weizen are similar to those for a Hefe Weizen, the taste and aroma of this beer are akin to those of its turbid relative. Kristall Weizen has seen its greatest popularity in Austria and other countries outside Germany that produce filtered Weissbier. It is not the beer of choice in Bavaria where Hefe Weizen is truly king. Nonetheless, many Bavarian breweries produce the yeastless variation of Weissbier, which seems to have been a great source of inspiration for brewers in North America.

The process steps involved in brewing a Kristall Weissbier are much the same as those for Hefe Weissbier, but more attention must be paid to the factors influencing the color, flavor and chemical-physical stability of this beer style. Unlike its yeasty cousin, once Kristall Weizen is in the bottle it is no longer alive and has achieved its prime. To attain a color of 3.5 to 5.0 SRM units (8 to 12 EBC units), only the palest barley and wheat malts are used. The brewing water is decarbonated so that a low residual alkalinity is created, which keeps the mash pH low. A low mash pH reduces the extraction of polyphenols from the barley husks, minimizing the risk of intensifying the color. Maintaining the proper pH in the mash will also aid the flavor of the finished beer, as an increased concentration of husk polyphenols will lend the beer a rough taste.[8] Boiling times for the decoctions are kept to a minimum (10 to 15 minutes) in the interest of a pale color.

The beer's resistance to chill haze is largely dependent upon the intensity of the brewhouse work. Single or double decoction mashes that emphasize protein rests sufficiently break down the higher molecular weight proteins in the mash-tun. Boiling the wort for at least two hours will help to precipitate the coagulable proteins out of solution, which further increases the beer's chemical-physical stability. However, boiling the wort excessively long is undesirable, as this deepens the color of the beer. Once again a low mash pH is helpful; in this case to aid protein coagulation. To further reduce the possibility of beer haze, many breweries stabilize the beer with bentonite or silicic acid derivatives, prior to or during filtration.

The primary fermentation of a Kristall Weizen is very similar to that of a Hefe Weizen, but there is a considerable difference in how the young beer is handled after it leaves the fermentation cellar. Because Kristall Weizen is not bottle conditioned, the maturation process takes place in tanks housed in a storage cellar. The tanks are cooled either by the ambient air temperature or with cooling jackets on each individual tank. The tanks must be able to withstand the high pressures that result from the secondary fermentation. The bunging pressure is set on the pressure relief valves so that the desired CO_2 content in the beer is reached during this phase of conditioning. Pressures of 3 to 5 atm. are set at a temperature of 54 to 61 degrees F (12 to 17 degrees C)[9] for a CO_2 content of 3.6 to 5.1 volumes (0.7 to 1.0 percent by weight).

If *Speise* (wort, kraeusen, or priming sugar used for carbonation) is being used, it is pumped into the storage tank prior to or at the same time as the young beer. As is the case with Hefe Weissbier, the amount of Speise to be used is calculated based on the desired CO_2 content of the beer. If a brewery does not have tanks that can withstand the high pressure of the secondary fermentation, the beer can be artificially carbonated later in the process. However, as is the law for all German beers, only CO_2 that has been obtained from a CO_2 recovery system in that particular brewery may be used to this end. The secondary fermentation is usually vigorous, and after a few hours the bunging pressure is reached.[10] The Speise extract is usually fermented within three days. Afterward a one-day diacetyl rest can be employed if neccessary.

If Speise is not being used, the young beer is fermented until the hydrometer reads about 2 °Plato more than the final gravity. It is then transferred into secondary tanks at a temperature of 59 to 64 degrees F (15 to 18 degrees C). The yeast cell count should be 50 million cells/mL[11] to ensure an intensive secondary fermentation. The temperature of the storage room and secondary fermenter is kept at 50 to 59 degrees F (10 to 15 degrees C). This warm storage stage usually requires seven to 10 days.[12]

Cold lagering the Kristall Weizen smooths and conditions the beer, and helps the artificial clarification process (i.e., filtering or centrifuging) that will follow, by allowing time for yeast and proteins to sediment out of the beer. The beer is transferred to a third vessel where it remains for at least 10 days. Again, either jacketed or air-cooled tanks are used to cool the beer to the desired temperature. The initial temperature of this second conditioning phase is 50 to 54 degrees F (10 to 12 degrees C). One to 2 percent bottom-fermenting kraeusen beer is added to the beer to continue the fermentation activity. The beer is cooled from this temperature to 32 degrees F (0 degrees C) within a week, and it remains at this temperature for one to two weeks.[13]

The Kristall Weizen is by now quite clear, but it still is filtered to achieve its brilliantly clear, pale golden color. The beer is usually easy to filter because it has been transferred so many times.[14] Because the beer has a greater than normal concentration of high molecular weight proteins, it may be necessary to increase the chemical-physical stability of the beer with Bentonite or silicic acid preparations. The filtered Kristall Weizen must be at a low temperature—34 to 36 degrees F (1 to 2 degrees C)—for the bottling to run smoothly,[15] due to the higher than normal CO_2 concentration of this beer style. Once the beer has been bottled, it is ready for sale.

- Leichtes Weissbier -

Original Gravity: 1.028-1.032 (7-8 °Plato)
Apparent Final Gravity: 1.006 (1.4-1.6 °Plato)
Apparent Degree of Attenuation: 79.9-82.7%
Real Degree of Attenuation: 64.7-67.0%
pH: 4.01-4.23
Bitterness: 13.0-16.5 IBU
Color: 2.7-4.6 SRM units (6-11 EBC units)
Alcohol Content: 3.0-3.4% v/v; 2.4-2.7% w/v
Calories per 12 oz. Serving: 93-102 (262-286 kcal/1,000 g)

Germany is not exempt from the worldwide trend of

making light lagers, and several wheat beer breweries have taken it upon themselves to produce reduced calorie, lower alcohol Weissbiers. As could be expected, the taste of these beers is less than overwhelming, but such is life for a light beer. Inspired more by acute awareness of individual responsibility when driving, and by the stiff penalties imposed for drunk driving offenses, German breweries brew their light beers to be lower alcohol beers, unlike the light beers in North America, which are marketed to the diet conscious and the "physically fit."

Unlike their North American counterparts, the German brewers of light wheat beers attempt to bring some kind of body, flavor and color into their product. One of the easiest ways to achieve these characteristics is to add 5 to 10 percent light or dark dextrin or "Cara-" malt to the grist. Using 60 to 70 percent wheat malt in the grist also helps increase the body of the Leichtes Weissbier. Finally, a decoction mash program in which boil times may be extended to 40 minutes for the decoction mashes also benefits the body and the color of the beer.

Ultimately, however, the overall character of the beer is diluted. Thus, any off flavors are more easily perceived in a light Weissbier than in a wheat beer of a higher starting gravity. It is very important that the overall character of the light Weizen be smooth, and to this end more attention is paid to the carbonate hardness of the brewing water, and to the pH of the mash and the kettle wort. Brewers of Leichtes Weissbier decarbonate their brewing water to minimize the acidity-reducing qualities of the carbonate ions. They may also adjust the mash and wort pH with calcium salts or with lactic acid that has been derived from a biological mash acidification. A process that is gaining in popularity among brewers all across Germany, the biological mash acidification lowers the mash pH to an optimal level for the primary enzymatic reactions in the mash. Beers that have been produced using a biological mash acidification consistently score well in blind taste tests, and the overall taste and quality of light beers, both lager and wheat, seem to benefit significantly from this practice.

To maintain the overall Weizenlike impression of the light wheat beers, brewers rarely strive for a bitterness greater than 15 IBU, and those beers that have a bitterness of 10 to 12 IBU seem to be received most favorably in blind taste tests. Because the yeast itself also contributes to the flavor of Leichtes Weissbier, most breweries produce their light beers with yeast in the bottle.[16] Lager yeasts or bottom-fermenting kraeusen beer is used for bottle conditioning. Top-fermenting yeasts are more susceptible to autolysis, which can give the beer a moldy, earthy taste or a harsh bitterness.[17]

As if light Weissbiers were too filling and incapacitating, and in keeping with the market trends in Germany, a couple of breweries have taken it upon themselves to introduce alcohol-free Weissbier to the world. To be worthy of that distinction, such a brew must contain less than 0.5 percent alcohol by weight, according to German law. These beers are brewed with a starting gravity of between 1.028 and 1.032 (7 and 8 °Plato) and the alcohol content is kept low by using the traditional methods of brewing such beverages (e.g., vacuum-distillation, dialysis, cold-contact process, fermenting with low attenuating yeasts, etc.). I have yet to try one of these brews, so I really don't know how they taste, but I'm not losing any sleep over it. This is one form of Weissbier that probably *does* taste better with a lemon slice in it.

- Berliner Weisse -

Original Gravity: 1.028-1.032 (7-8 °Plato)
Apparent Final Gravity: 1.002-1.006 (0.5-1.6 °Plato)
Apparent Degree of Attenuation: 80-94%

Real Degree of Attenuation: 65-76%
pH: 3.2-3.4
Bitterness: 4-6 IBU
Color: 2.0-3.5 SRM units (4-8 EBC units)
Alcohol Content: 2-3% w/v; 2.5-3.8% v/v
Calories per 12 oz. serving: 92-99 (260-280 kcal/1,000 g)

Dubbed "the Champagne of the north" by Napoleon's soldiers in 1809, Berliner Weisse, like its cousins in the south, is enjoying a bit of a renaissance in the German beer market. This is the most tart and thirst-quenching of all the German wheat beers, in part due to its lower starting gravity, but mainly because a symbiotic lactic acid fermentation complements the yeast fermentation. The result is a light, refreshing and effervescent beer that is served as a summer specialty, but can be enjoyed at any time of the year. To cut the sharp acidity of Berliner Weisse dashes of raspberry syrup, essence of woodruff, or *Kümmel* (caraway) schnapps can be added. True Berliners know that the best cure for the common cold is a hot Berliner Weisse with lemon juice!

The first documented evidence of Berliner Weisse production is in 1680. As with the southern Weissbier, it was necessary to pay a special tax for the right to brew it. Pub owners buried clay bottles of Berliner Weisse in the cellar with sand to prevent them from exploding. The bottles would rest in peace for a year beneath the sand and then the beer would be served without the yeast sediment. At the time of Napoleon's visit to Berlin, the Weisse was being served in giant three-liter glass tubs. In order to successfully imbibe the beer, a helper was required to hold the giant glass. This vessel evolved into a more manageable large, flat goblet, and then into the current Berliner Weisse glass, which is similar to a beer schooner.

Only brewers in Berlin can use the term Berliner Weisse

for their beers, just as the term Kölsch is reserved for brewers in the Cologne region. Breweries in other parts of Germany may brew this style of beer, but they must label it as "wheat beer, Berlin style" or something of that nature. Unlike the wheat beers in Southern Germany, Berliner Weisse is classified as *Schankbier*, meaning that its starting gravity must be between 1.028 and 1.032 (7 and 8 °Plato) according to the German beer tax law. Naturally, the low starting gravity means that the alcohol content is quite low, about 3.1 percent by volume (2.5 percent by weight). In earlier times the amount of wheat malt in the grist was as low as 25 to 30 percent,[18] but today it ranges from 50 to 75 percent. Berliner Weisse is hopped even less than the Weissbiers of the south, with between 4 and 6 IBU. Because of the lactic fermentation of Berliner Weisse, the pH of the beer can be as low as 3, and the content of lactic acid can be as high as 0.8 percent.[19] The CO_2 content of Berliner Weisse is similar to that of Hefe Weissbier, although values higher than 4.1 volumes (0.8 percent by weight) are uncommon.

Medium hard to hard waters are used to brew Berliner Weisse and, although two or three decoction mashes used to be standard practice, an infusion mash program is the norm today.[20] Traditionally the hops were added to the mash, which helped the lautering process some by loosening the mash.[21] Today the hops are added to the kettle wort, which may or may not be brought to a full boil, depending on the brewery. Originally the wort was taken directly from the lauter-tun and cooled in a cooling ship, then the yeast culture was pitched, completely bypassing a boiling of the wort.[22] A more recent development is to heat the wort to 185 to 190 degrees F (85 to 88 degrees C) to sterilize it.[23]

The key to the essence of a Berliner Weisse is the lactic acid fermentation that complements the yeast fermentation. The culture yeast contains a certain amount of lactic acid bacteria, usually in a ratio of four to six parts yeast to one part lactic acid bacteria.[24] These are not just any lactic acid bacteria, but *Lactobacillus delbrückii*, appropriately named after Professor Max Delbrück, the prolific professor at the world-famous brewing university and research station in Berlin who isolated this particular strain. It is essential that fermentation temperatures be kept below 68 degrees F (20 degrees C) to control the production of lactic acid. Higher concentrations of lactic acid will hinder the yeast's performance and drastically alter the spectrum of fermentation byproducts. At the Schultheiss brewery in Berlin, the wort is pitched and blended with three- to six-month-old beer. Once the fermentation is underway, the lactic acid bacteria rise to the surface and are harvested in traditional fashion along with the top-fermenting yeast. The yeast is repitched as quickly as possible, because the amount of lactic acid will rise within a few days to concentrations that will inhibit not only the yeast, but the lactic acid bacteria themselves. Although the wort is relatively weak and normal fermentation temperatures are used, it takes about four days for the wort to attenuate to the desired degree because of the inhibiting effect the lactic acid has on the yeast. Unlike Hefe Weissbier, Berliner Weisse is not completely attenuated in the fermentation cellar; rather, it is attenuated to about 80 percent of its limit.[25]

There is no set manner in which the conditioning of

Berliner Weisse takes place, but all methods use a form of kraeusening to aid the maturation of the beer. The faster of these methods involves adding about 10 percent kraeusen to the young beer in a mixing tank just prior to bottling. After bottling, the beer is subjected to a warm secondary fermentation at approximately 59 degrees F (15 degrees C) before it is cooled to 46 to 50 degrees F (8 to 10 degrees C) for the cold conditioning.[26] Again, as is the case with other styles of Weissbier, the warm conditioning phase serves to jump-start the secondary fermentation and develop the CO_2 in the beer. Berliner Weisse produced in this manner is ready for distribution after a total production time of about five weeks.

According to Michael Jackson in his *World Guide to Beer*, the Schulteiss brewery believes that this time frame is much too limiting to allow the beer to develop its full character. After the primary fermentation the beer spends three to 12 months in the conditioning cellar at very warm temperatures of 59 to 77 degrees F (15 to 25 degrees C). These temperatures promote the lactic acid fermentation, which results in an extremely low pH of 3.0 and an incredibly high apparent degree of attenuation of 98.4 percent.[27] The beer is then kraeusened prior to bottling and, as if the lactic quality weren't enhanced enough, another dose of *Lactobacillus delbrückii* is added to the primed Weisse. The Schulteiss Weisse is then stored in the bottle at temperatures of 64 to 77 degrees F (18 to 25 degrees C) for four weeks before it is released for sale.

Berliner Weisse is a rare example of a beer that can be stored by the consumer or publican for a virtually unlimited amount of time. Whereas it is unthinkable to store a Hefe Weissbier of standard gravity for two years, a Berliner Weisse will just be entering its prime after 18 months, displaying a lovely balance of fruitiness, lactic acidity and quenching tartness. Stored bottles of Berliner Weisse should be kept at temperatures of 43 to 50 degrees F (6 to 10 degrees C).

Like the Hefe Weissbier in the south, Berliner Weisse has enormous potential for the future. Now that Berlin is again the official capital of Germany, it will experience immense growth and an even greater volume of tourists than it has in the past, and will once again become one of the great political and cultural centers of Europe. Ah yes, to stroll down the famous Kudamm on a warm summer's eve, having just taken in a show, and then to enjoy a schooner of Weisse at an outdoor café, that is Berlin!

- The Other Wheat Beers of Germany -

The Bremer Weisse from Bremen is quite similar to the Berliner Weisse, but is not as acidic. Bremer Weisse is made by the Haake-Beck Brauerei in Bremen, known in the United States for its "Beck's," "Beck's Light," and "Beck's Dark" labels. Bremer Weisse has a much higher pH (3.6) than the average Berliner Weisse, which is mainly attributable to the lower levels of lactic acid. The Bremer Weisse contains about 1,100 mg/L of L- and D-lactate, whereas the Schulteiss Weisse from Berlin has a combined total of more than 5,500 mg/L of lactates.[28] Also a Schankbier, the Bremer Weisse has a starting gravity of about 1.032 (8 °Plato), but because it is not as fully attenuated as the Schulteiss, its alcohol content is a bit less, at 3.0 percent by volume (2.4 percent by weight).[29, 30] Bremer Weisse is also more liberally hopped than Berliner Weisse, but at only 12 IBU the difference is hardly noticeable.[31] Like Berliner Weisse, Bremer Weisse is also often enjoyed with a dash of fruit syrup, and is very thirst-quenching and refreshing. The city of Hanover was also once known for its wheat beers, but unfortunately these products are extinct.

3

Physical and Chemical Composition

Note: unless otherwise specified, the information in this chapter pertains to pale Hefe Weissbier.

CARBONATION

Perhaps the most striking quality of Weissbier is its high degree of carbonation. German lagers may have a CO_2 content of 2.3 volumes (0.45 percent by weight), and American lagers may be slightly higher, but Weissbiers are even more effervescent. Levels range from 2.8 to 5.1 volumes (0.55 to 1.0 percent by weight),[32] with the average being around 3.9 volumes (0.75 percent by weight). Weissbiers at the higher end of the scale tend to be too gassy, and it is easy to become bloated by drinking just one of them. I prefer beers that have a CO_2 content of less than 3.6 volumes (0.7 percent by weight), but many of the most popular Weissbiers in Germany have a level that is higher.

STARTING GRAVITY AND ALCOHOL CONTENT

The starting gravity of Weissbier can be anywhere from

1.044 to 1.056 (11 to 14 °Plato), with most of the well known Weissbiers weighing in at 1.049 to 1.055 (12.3 to 13.8 °Plato). If the starting gravity is greater than 1.050 (12.5 °Plato) the brewery may choose to label the beer Export Weissbier. Confusion can arise when talking about alcohol content, because it is defined in two ways. German Weissbier consumers will read "Vol. %" on Weissbier labels. However, the unit of measure that brewers use is percent by weight. With apparent degrees of attenuation that can range from 78 to 86 percent, Hefe Weissbier contains a moderate level of alcohol, ranging from 5.0 to 5.6 percent by volume (4.0 to 4.5 percent by weight).

COLOR

The color of a pale Weissbier is 3.5 to 6.1 SRM units (8 to 15 EBC units), although some breweries may brew a Weissbier with a color as high as 11.7 SRM units (30 EBC units) without touting it as a Dunkles Weissbier. Dark Weissbiers or Weizenbocks have a color that ranges from 10 to 23 SRM units (25 to 60 EBC units). By comparison, German light lagers have a color range of 3.1 to 4.6 SRM units (7 to 11 EBC units),[33] and American lagers may be even lower. A Hefe Weizen, once it has been poured into a glass, has a pale, opaque gold color that might have a slight brown or orange tinge to it.

PH

As is the case with all top-fermented beers, the pH of a Weissbier is usually in the range of 4.0 to 4.4. German lagers have a pH somewhere between 4.4 and 4.6, with American lagers being less than 4.4 but more than 4.0. If the pH of a Weissbier is less than 4, it is not unreasonable to assume that some sort of lactic infection is present. Some Weizen beers do have a pH lower than 4, and have a slightly sour, lactic taste that is not at all unpleasant, but if the pH is less than 3.6, the beer is quite sour and untrue to the style (other wheat beers, such as Lambic or Berliner Weisse, have a pH lower than 3.6, but these beers are of an entirely different character and makeup than the wheat beers of Southern Germany and Austria). If the pH of a Weissbier is greater than 4.4, it usually indicates autolysis or the excretion of basic amino acids. This can happen if the beer has been stored in the bottle for a long time, or if it has been subjected to high temperatures. If top-fermenting yeast is used for bottle conditioning, the tendency toward autolysis increases. Finally, the brewhouse work also can affect the pH of the finished product. If the wort is deficient in amino nitrogen or fermentable sugars, the pH reduction during the fermentation may be sluggish. This is rarely the case, however, because top-fermenting yeasts are less sensitive to wort pH than lager yeasts.

BITTERNESS

The bitterness of a Weissbier ranges from 6 to 18 IBU[34] with the most typical values being around 12 to 15 IBU. At least 30 mg/L of alpha acid should be dosed into the wort simply for the bacteriostatic insurance that hops give the beer.[35] If the Weissbier contains more than 18 IBU it will have an undesirable bitterness, particularly if low-grade, high-alpha hops were used.

FLAVOR AND AROMA

The most commonly used word by the millions of armchair braumeisters in Germany to describe the flavor and aroma of Weissbier is *würzig,* or spicy. Another common term is *nelkenartig* (clovelike). To brewers and brewing scientists these words are synonymous with phenolic. Although the esters and alcohols play an important role in the elegant balance of Weissbier flavor and aroma, it is the phenolic substances in Bavarian and Swabian wheat beers that set them apart from any other beers in the world.

If one compound had to be isolated for its abililty to produce the typical flavor and aroma on the taste of Hefe Weissbier, it would have to be the phenolic substance 4-vinyl guaiacol.[36] Its aroma is most commonly described as clovelike. Nonetheless, the other phenolic substances present in Weissbier, particularly 4-vinyl phenol, also greatly influence the character of the finished beer, and in some cases may completely overshadow the flavor and aroma of the 4-vinyl guaiacol. The primary representative of the p-cumaric acid derivatives is 4-vinyl phenol. Others include 4-hydroxy benzaldehyde, which is phenolically bitter; and phenol, which is phenolic and cresollike. A derivative of sinapinic acid, 4-vinyl syringol has a smoky aroma and flavor, but this characteristic is not always typical for Weissbier.

Still other phenolic substances also contribute to the complex bouquet of this beer style. Guaiacol, a derivative of ferulic acid (as is 4-vinyl guaiacol), has a phenolic, medicinal character. Vanillin and acetovanillon give the impression of, you guessed it, vanilla. Although these two compounds rarely dominate the character of a Weizenbier, their presence is perceptible in some cases. Isoeugenol has a clovelike and nutmeglike aroma. It is easy to understand why the word spicy is often used to describe the palate and bouquet of a Weissbier. The most interesting Weissbiers are those that display a balance of all the phenolic substances, leaving the drinker grasping for words to describe the complex and intricate spectrum of phenols.

Phenolic substances in Weissbier are usually isolated using gas chromatography, but colorometric and thin layer chromatographic methods are also used. The level of 4-vinyl guaiacol can range from virtually nil to over 4,000 ppb. The threshold level of perception is approximately 800 ppb. Levels of 4-vinyl guaiacol close to the high end of the range quite possibly indicate an infection.[37] In one study, Weissbiers containing 1,500 to 2,500 ppb were preferred by brewing professionals in Germany, but this preference was contingent upon the content of other phenolic substances in the Weissbier.[38] If the concentration of 4-vinyl phenol exceeded 1,500 ppb or if the concentrations of 4-methyl guaiacol, 4-ethyl guaiacol or eugenol were high, the beers were judged less favorably.[39] Yeast strains that produce less than 700 ppb of 4-vinyl guaiacol yield neutral, bland-tasting Hefe Weissbiers that are not typical of the style.[40]

By far the most important influence on the development of phenolic substances is the yeast strain used. Only a few strains are capable of producing the high levels of phenolic substances found in Weissbier. One strain is used almost exclusively in the Weissbier breweries of southern Germany, though other strains have been tested that are capable of producing phenols in concentrations that are almost double those produced by the commonly used yeast strain.[41]

Fermentation temperature also plays a significant role in developing phenolic substances. As a rule, the higher the fermentation temperature, the higher the amounts of 4-vinyl guaiacol and 4-vinyl phenol in the finished beer.[42] If the fermentation temperature is raised from 59 to 68 degrees F (15 degrees C to 20 degrees C), the amount of 4-vinyl guaiacol can increase by almost 50 percent, and if the beer ferments at 77 degrees F (25 degrees C) the increase will be almost 75 percent.[43] These results were obtained from small-scale laboratory fermentations that yielded two more interesting results. One was that the Weissbier fermented at the lower temperature (68 degrees F, 20 degrees C) developed the most 4-vinyl guaiacol and 4-vinyl phenol during the *primary* fermentation, but the beer fermented at the higher temperature (77 degrees F, 25 degrees C) had the highest absolute concentration of these compounds at the end of the *entire* fermentation process (i.e., after bottle conditioning). Second, after the Speise was added to the beer, the rate of increase slowed and actually began to *decrease* after seven days. A possible explanation for the decrease is that the yeast absorbed some of these substances once the maturation phase began.

The specific conditions present in each individual brewery also seem to have an impact on the development of phenolic substances in Weissbier. The type of fermenter used is particularly influential. Research indicates that open fermentation yields the highest levels of the two primary aroma phenols in Weissbier. Even when the fermentation temperatures were similar, the beers fermented in cylindroconical tanks usually had lower levels of 4-vinyl guaiacol and 4-vinyl phenol than those fermented in open fermenters.[44] The reasons for these differences are presently unknown, but one possible explanation is that the washing effect of the CO_2 in the cylindro-conical tank is greater due to the increased ratio of fermenter height to beer surface area, as compared to open-batch fermenters.

Further process steps that seem to reduce the phenol content of Weissbier are cold trub flotation and clarification of the green beer. Cold trub flotation may separate the precursors to the phenols from the wort, particularly if flotation takes place without yeast.[45] Decreases in phenolic substances have been observed after the green beer was filtered or centrifuged.[46] The highest levels of 4-vinyl guaiacol and 4-vinyl phenol are reached by using open fermenters and warm fermentation temperatures, and by priming with Speise.[47]

Contrary to popular belief, the percentage of wheat malt used in the grist has little influence on the concentrations of phenolic substances found in Hefe Weissbier. It is true that barley malt has a lower concentration of phenol carbonic acids (the precursors to phenolic substances) than wheat malt, but the absolute amount is still sufficient for a strong development of phenolic substances.[48] The highest concentrations of 4-vinyl guaiacol seem to be found when one-third wheat malt is used in the grist.[49]

Weissbier also is characterized by a higher content of fusel and aromatic alcohols than is found in lager beers. The concentration of higher alcohols in German lagers is normally between 60 and 90 mg/L,[50] while in Weissbier the sum of the higher alcohols ranges from 110 to 170 mg/L.[51] Lagers average about 20 mg/L of phenyl ethanol[52] while a Weizenbier may have as much as 65 mg/L,[53] which is in the threshold range of perceptibility. These differences are not surprising, as top-fermenting yeasts produce more fusel and aromatic alcohols than bottom-fermenting yeasts. This is partly because of the nature of top-fermenting yeast itself, but also because top-fermenting beers ferment at higher temperatures, and fermentation temperature greatly influences the production of certain key higher alcohols. If the fermentation temperature is increased from 61 to 72 degrees F (16 to 22 degrees C), the amount of iso-butanol will increase by more than 50 percent[54] and the concentration of 2-phenyl ethanol will increase by almost 70 percent.[55] Phenyl ethanol has a flowery, roselike smell, and is not at all uncommon in a Weissbier. Weissbier yeast in particular produces more of these alcohols than yeasts used for other top-fermented German beers such as alt and Kölsch.[56]

The concentration of esters in top-fermented beers may be as much as 50 percent higher than that of bottom-fermented beers. The ester content of a Weissbier can range from 21 to 40 mg/L.[57] The concentration is dependent on the type of fermenter used—cylindro-conical tanks produce only two-thirds the concentration of esters found in open fermenters.[58] This difference seems to be a function of convection: the stronger the convection in the cylindro-conical fermenter, the lower the ester content is.

One of the more common and desirable esters in a Weissbier is iso-amyl acetate. This ester contributes a banana- or candylike aroma to the beer, and is the trademark of selected Weissbiers in the Munich area. Present normally in concentrations of only 1.5 mg/L in German lagers, isoamyl acetate may exceed 5 mg/L in a Hefe Weissbier.[59] Most Hefe Weissbiers have at least 2.0 mg/L of the banana ester, which is at the low end of the perceptibility threshold. If you think someone has mistakenly placed a banana slice in your Weissbier instead of a lemon slice, check again—it may just be part of the inherent aroma of the beer. Other fruity or flowery impressions you may perceive could be a result of increased ethyl acetate concentrations, which are also considerably higher in Weissbier.

The vicinal diketones rarely present a problem in Weissbier. As is true with all top-fermented beers, 2-aceto lactate develops more rapidly and in greater amounts than in lager beers, but in Weissbier the reduction to diacetyl is also more rapid. This is even more pronounced with higher fermentation temperatures. The reduction of diacetyl to the threshold level has usually occurred by the time the bottles are switched from the warm conditioning phase to the cold phase. In other words, it is not at all unthinkable that the concentration of diacetyl can be reduced to less than 0.12 mg/L in seven to 10 days. The addition of the Speise and yeast or kraeusen mixture is added insurance against the threat of threshold concentrations of diacetyl. It is rare for a Weissbier to contain more than 0.1mg/L diacetyl after it has been fully conditioned. The average German Weizen beer contains 0.03 mg/L diacetyl;[60] if the level is greater than 0.1 mg/L, either grave errors were made in the brewing and fermenting process steps, or an infection is present.

The spectrum of organic acids in Weissbier is very similar to that in lager beers with the exception of lactate. In German bottom-fermented beers the amount of D- and L-lactate is usually less than 100 mg/L for each compound,[61] but some Weissbiers may contain as much as 165 mg/L of D-lactate.[62] Some of the more popular Weissbiers are noted for their slightly sour, quenching taste. Nonetheless, these levels are still relatively low; Berliner Weisse (see Chapter 6) can contain as much as 3,000 mg/L of each lactate, and some lambics have more than 10,000 mg/L![63]

Acetaldehyde develops considerably more in Weissbier than in lagers as the fermentation comes into its peak, but its subsequent decrease during the rest of the primary fermentation also is much more dramatic, so that the absolute amount is usually less than in bottom-fermented beers. It is a rare occasion that somebody returns a Weissbier claiming that it has a young beer taste.

COMPOSITION

The following composition table (Table 1) for pale Weissbiers is divided into three sections. Section 1 is a compilation of analysis data from the German publication *Brauindustrie*, in which 10 different Weissbiers were analyzed.[64] This section provides information from the more basic analyses such as starting gravity, bitterness, color and alcohol content. Section 2 presents results of gas chromatography analysis of the volatile compounds in 60 different Weissbiers (beers that were submitted for the yearly judging at the Technical University of Munich, Weihenstephan.[65] Section 3 combines data from section 2 and, where marked with an asterisk, from another analysis of the phenolic content of 22 Weissbiers.[66] In all cases one thing is clear: the variation of values among most substances, particularly the volatiles, is great. This variation cannot be attributed to inaccuracy or imprecision in analytical methods or laboratories used to evaluate the beers; it is an indication of the wide spectrum of brewing procedures and ingredients employed to brew the Weissbiers in question. In all three sections the mean and the range of values are given.

TABLE 1
Section 1: Primary composition

	Mean	Xmin	Xmax
Original extract, g/100 g (specific gravity)	12.70 (1.051)	11.90 (1.049)	13.80 (1.056)
Real extract, g/100 g (real final gravity)	4.20 (1.017)	3.70 (1.015)	4.90 (1.020)
Apparent degree of fermentation, %	82.60	80.10	85.60
Real degree of fermentation, %	66.90	64.90	69.30
Apparent limit of attenuation, %	82.80	80.10	85.70
Alcohol, g/100 g	4.22	3.96	4.53
Caloric content, kcal/1,000 g (i.e., calories per liter)	456.00	424.00	499.00
pH	4.32	4.23	4.50
Bitterness, IBU	13.50	10.50	19.00
Dissolved carbon dioxide, g/100 g (volumes)	0.77 (4.00)	0.64 (3.30)	0.87 (4.50)
Color, EBC units (SRM units)	13.00 (5.30)	8.30 (3.60)	24.00 (9.50)
Raw protein (sol. N x 6.25), Kjeldahl method, g/L	5.30	4.40	7.10
Free amino nitrogen, TNBS method, mg/L	88.00	54.00	120.00
Viscosity, cP	1.77	1.69	1.87
Total polyphenols, mg/L	93.00	53.00	132.00
Anthocyanogenes, mg/L	23.00	12.00	40.00
Minerals, mg/L			
Potassium	444.00	370.00	566.00
Sodium	24.00	10.00	80.00

Calcium	27.00	14.00	70.00
Magnesium	83.00	74.00	98.00
Phosphorus	315.00	256.00	387.00
Sulfate	120.00	80.00	195.00
Chloride	127.00	100.00	153.00
Nitrate	20.00	5.00	85.00
Iron	0.17	0.07	0.35
Zinc	0.06	0.01	0.18
Vitamins, µg/L			
Thiamine	145.00	17.00	592.00
Riboflavin	375.00	275.00	437.00
Pantothenic acid	1706.00	1306.00	1986.00
Niacin	7304.00	6300.00	9000.00
Organic acids, mg/L			
Pyruvate	56.00	11.00	82.00
Citrate	146.00	130.00	168.00
Malate	78.00	58.00	97.00
L-Lactate	27.00	10.00	90.00
D-Lactate	75.00	36.00	135.00

Section 2: Secondary Composition and Flavor-Influencing Fermentation Byproducts

(In mg/L unless otherwise indicated)

	Mean	Xmin	Xmax	Typical Concentration	Characteristic Flavor or Aroma	Threshold level in German lagers
Acetaldehyde	0.40	0.10	1.40	5.00-10.00	acidic, slightly fruity, pungent	
Total Diacetyl	0.04	0.02	0.47	<0.20	buttery, butterscotch	0.10-0.15
Acetoin	3.10	1.10	33.10	2.00-3.00		8.00-20.00
HIGHER ALCOHOLS						
Propanol-1	18.80	11.30	52.10	6.00-9.00	fusel, solventlike	
2-methyl propanol-1	36.50	19.80	59.80	5.00-10.00	fusel, solventlike	> 10.00
2-methyl butanol-1 (amyl alcohol)	20.10	13.80	82.60	**	fusel, solventlike	20.00-70.00
3-methyl butanol-1 (isoamyl alcohol)	58.00	41.00	102.00	**	fusel, solventlike	20.00-70.00

** The sum of the amyl alcohols is 40-60 mg/L

49

2-phenyl ethanol
33.00	13.00	64.00	5.00-20.00	rose or rose oil	> 30.00

ESTERS

Ethyl acetate
32.00	13.00	54.00	5.00-25.00	solventlike (acetone) in reduced concentrations, flowery	25.00-30.00

Isoamyl acetate
4.00	0.70	9.00	0.50-2.00	very fruity, banana	1.00-1.60

Hexanoic acid ethyl ester (ethyl caproate)
0.12	0.06	0.20	0.10-0.30	fruity, winy	0.12-0.23

Octanoic acid ethyl ester (ethyl caprylate)
0.25	0.04	0.37	0.10-0.50	fruity, winy	> 0.20

Decanoic acid ethyl ester (ethyl caprate)
0.05	0.01	0.26	< 0.05	fruity, winy	

Acetic acid 2-phenyl ethyl ester (phenyl ethyl acetate)
0.98	0.09	2.24	0.20-1.00	rose or honey	

FATTY ACIDS

Butyric acid	0.09	0.01	0.50	0.20-0.60	rancid	1.20-2.20
Isovaleric acid	1.30	0.80	4.50	0.50-1.20		1.50-1.60
Caproic acid	2.20	0.40	6.20	< 8.00	goaty, yeasty	
Caprylic acid	4.70	2.40	7.50	3.00-8.00	goaty, yeasty	10.00-13.00
Capric acid	0.60	0.10	1.90	< 1.50	goaty, yeasty	10.00

Dimethyl sulfide (DMS), µg/L
42.00	17.00	81.00	20-80 µg/L	cooked vegetable, creamed corn	50-80 µg/L

Section 3: Content of Phenolic Substances, µg/L

	Characteristics	Mean	Xmin	Xmax
Phenol	phenolic, cresollike	40	+	110
Guaiacol	phenolic, medicinal	120	+	360
4-vinyl phenol	strongly phenolic	970	10	7,390
4-vinyl guaiacol	clovelike	1,500	280	3,710
Eugenol*	phenolic	70	+	215
Isoeugenol*	clovelike, nutmeglike	38	+	156
4-vinyl syringol*	smoky	310	96	586
4-hydroxy benzaldehyde*	phenolically bitter	125	+	318
Aceto vanillone*	vanillalike	153	+	474

* Data from an analysis of the phenolic content of 22 Weissbiers.

4

Brewing a Weissbier

WHEAT MALT

Barley malt is used extensively in the worldwide brewing and distilling industries, so certain strains of barley have been developed to meet the needs of brewers and distillers. Because wheat is grown primarily for use in the food industries, agricultural research has focused on developing new wheat strains for their qualities as a flour or feed, not to fulfill the ideal requirements of a brewer. The biggest compromise a wheat beer brewer must make is to accept a cereal grain that has a higher than desired protein content. A maltmaster is lucky to be able to work with raw wheat that has less than 12 percent protein, and often this figure is exceeded.

Winter wheat is preferable to summer wheat because of its lower protein content, which translates to higher extract values of the malt and paler colors in the beer.[67] The higher protein content of wheat malt and the structure of wheat proteins are a mixed blessing to the brewer who chooses to make a wheat beer. The protein fractions in barley are roughly 5 percent albumins, 30 percent globulins, 30 percent prolamines and 35 percent glutelines.[68] In wheat, roughly 80 percent of the proteins are glutens, and the rest is albumin and globulin.[69] Another difference between the protein structure of barley and wheat is in their respective aleurone layers. In barley, thick-walled cells comprised of protein and fat form a triple layer,[70] whereas the aleurone layer of wheat is only one cell thick.[71] Because there are proportionately more higher molecular weight proteins in wheat malt than in barley malt, wheat beers often build foam better than beers made exclusively from barley malt. However, beers with a higher concentration of coagulable proteins often are susceptible to chill haze in the finished beer. If the beer has been filtered, stability problems may arise. The glutinous character of wheat proteins and wheat's lack of husks also cause problems in the lauter-tun, limiting the percentage of wheat that can be used in a brewhouse with a modern lauter-tun to about 70 percent.

A brewer should be hesitant to use wheat malts that do not meet the following criteria:

Extract, dry weight, percent	>83.0
Protein, dry weight, percent	<12.5
Fine/coarse grist difference, percent	<2.0

The wheat malt should also be free from discolored kernels. Such malts may be contaminated by fungi, and gushing problems may result. In particular, kernels that are red or purple have usually fallen victim to an attack of the Fusarium fungus. As a norm value, wheat (or barley for that matter) should not have more than three red kernels per 100 grams of sample. In 1987, following an extremely wet summer that resulted in a larger than normal incidence of Fusarium development in the harvested crops, there was an extreme problem with Weissbiers gushing. Studies have since linked the gushing phenomenon to the presence of Fusarium fungi in barley and wheat.

A Bavarian Brewmaster poses beside a copper mush-tun.

The preparation of wheat malt is similar to that of barley malt, though there are several noteworthy differences, most of which are attributable to the lower modification time of wheat. Because the small, round size of wheat kernels allows them to pack together tightly, the heat generated during germination is retained well by the grain pile, and modification is faster than with barley malt.[72] The huskless wheat kernels will also reach the desired degree of steeping quicker than barley, as the barley husks impede the kernels' uptake of water. The combination of these two factors allows the germination period to be reduced by one to two days compared to barley malt. Because modification is rapid, cooler germination temperatures are often used to control the modification process. Tracking the malting process for wheat yields two interesting observations. First, only one or two rootlets shoot out from each wheat kernel,[73] whereas the barley corn has several rootlets protruding from it. Second, the strength of the glutinous layer in wheat makes crumbling a modified kernel between thumb and forefinger (a reliable means of determining whether or not modification is complete in barley) much more difficult than with a barley corn, thereby complicating the empirical analysis of green wheat malt.

Wheat malts are kilned in much the same manner as barley malts; however, the withering process is slower and the kilning temperature is somewhat lower. Pale German barley malts are kilned at 176 to 185 degrees F (80 to 85 degrees C), while a pale wheat malt is kilned for about two hours at 167 degrees F (75 degrees C), then three hours at 176 degrees F (80 degrees C).[74] Despite its lower kilning temperature, much of the high molecular weight protein in wheat malts is coagulated.[75]

Table 2 highlights the differences between pale barley and pale wheat malts.

Table 2: Characteristics of Barley and Wheat Malts[76]

	Barley malt	Summer wheat malt	Winter wheat malt
Extract, air dry, %	80.50	83.40	85.00
Coarse grits/fine grits, extract difference, %	1.60	1.70	1.30
Protein, dry substance, %	11.00	14.20	13.10
Amino-N (Ninhydrin method), mg/100 g dry substance	140.00	161.00	132.00
Soluble nitrogen, mg/100 g dry substance	650.00	981.00	799.00
Color, EBC units	3.50	6.10	5.10
pH	5.90	6.06	6.06

The most striking difference between malts is the higher extract yield of the wheat malts. This factor has enabled wheat to be used in the mashes of beers around the world. Wheat is also less expensive than barley, with winter wheat prices at $1 to $2 less (per 100 weight) than those of malting barley. The unsuitability of summer wheat for the brewing process is not contingent upon its lower extract yield, but rather its extremely high protein content. If summer wheat was used for brewing Weissbier the amino-nitrogen contents of the worts could reach acceptable levels, but the increased amount of higher-molecular-weight proteins would cause chaos in the lauter-tun, the boil would have to be at least 135 minutes long for proper protein coagulation, and chill-haze problems would be likely.

Wheat malts yield worts that are slightly darker than barley malts. A pale barley malt should have a maximum color of 1.95 SRM units (4.0 EBC units), while a wheat malt made from winter wheat is usually at least 0.8 SRM units (1 EBC unit) darker. The increased protein levels of the wheat malts contribute to their higher color values. Wheat malt has more nitrogen compounds present in the green malt prior to kilning, so the color-deepening compounds that result from the browning reactions during the kilning process reach higher levels, even though wheat malt is kilned at a slightly lower temperature than barley malt.

BREWING WATER FOR WEISSBIER

The brewing water used for German style wheat beers can be soft, hard or anything in between. The variation is great among the wheat beer breweries in Germany—some use water with a hardness of almost 450 ppm $CaCO_3$ while others use water as low as 50 ppm.[77] The alkalinities of these waters are also quite diverse, but even a high carbonate hardness in water will have a less negative effect on a Weissbier than on a light lager. Top-fermenting yeasts are not as sensitive as are lager yeasts to wort pH, and the pH of a top-fermenting beer will plummet to 4.0 to 4.1 regardless of the pH of the cast-out wort.[78]

A typical water from the Munich area has the following composition (all values are expressed in ppm):

Total hardness	265
Alkalinity	255
Calcium hardness	190
Magnesium hardness	75
Sulfate (SO_4^{2-})	9
Chloride (Cl^-)	2

GRIST COMPOSITION

The *Reinheitsgebot*, the most notorious of all German brewing laws, requires that only **malted** wheat be used for a wheat beer (the law requires that only malted cereal grains be used for brewing any German beer). It is an unwritten law and a consumer expectation that a Weissbier be made with at least 50 percent wheat. This position is backed up by the German equivalent of the FDA, even though the German beer tax law (*Biersteuergesetz*) does not dictate what percentage of malted wheat a German wheat beer must contain.[79] Earlier wheat beers were made with 35 percent wheat, but improvements in milling and lautering technology have made it possible to increase that percentage. Now it is common for many breweries to brew wheat beers that contain as much as 70 percent wheat malt.[80]

Wheat malt can be either pale or dark, depending on the particular style of Weissbier. Light or dark cara malts are often added to the grist of pale Hefe Weissbiers to improve the body of the beer, but usually no more than 5 percent and 1 percent, respectively. If a dark wheat beer is being brewed, the desired color and aroma can be achieved by using dark barley malt, dark wheat malt, dark cara malt, colored beer or some combination thereof. If more than 70 percent wheat malt is used, both the wheat and the barley malt should be well modified to preclude the possibility of a set lauter mash. Conditioning the malts with steam just prior to milling, or grinding the grains with a wet milling system will help to keep the testa and pericarp of the wheat kernel intact,[81] thereby facilitating the development of a looser grain bed in the lauter-tun.

An amino acid deficiency, which can lead to weak fermentations and undesirable fermentation byproducts in the finished beer, may result if more than 70 percent wheat malt is used. It is important that all worts, not just Weizen worts, contain an appropriate level of amino acids. These

The new, ultra-modern brewhouse at the G. Schneider & Sohn Brewery. (See listing of breweries.)

are the fundamental building blocks of new yeast cells; if the wort has a lower than acceptable amount of amino acids, the fermentation may be sluggish, and unwanted byproducts such as diacetyl and fusel alcohols may develop in the beer. A wort also should not contain a greater than necessary concentration of amino acids, otherwise higher than normal concentrations of fusel alcohols will result.

Higher concentrations of wheat malt in the grist were associated with unacceptably low levels of amino nitrogen in the cast-out wort in a German study.[82] At a wheat malt to barley malt ratio of 40 to 60, the amino nitrogen content was at the low end of tolerability at 16.0 mg/100mL. When the researchers increased the wheat malt proportion to 80 percent, the amino nitrogen level dropped to 13.7 mg/100 mL, and, at 100 percent, the amino nitrogen content was just 11.7 mg/100mL. The viscosity of the 100 percent wheat malt wort was also more than 50 percent greater than the 100 percent barley malt wort.

MASH PROCEDURES

A single or double decoction mash is used when brewing a Weissbier wort for three main reasons. First, it supplies the yeast with an adequate amount of amino acids. Second, it breaks down the higher-molecular-weight proteins so that the runoff will not be impeded by doughy, glutinous substances. Third, this intensive breakdown of high molecular weight proteins reduces chill haze in the finished product, a phenomenon that is particularly undesirable in packaged beer and in filtered beers such as Kristall Weizen. Sufficient protein rests are also necessary to maximize the amino acid content of the wort and to reduce problematic higher-molecular-weight proteins. The protein problem with wheat beers is illustrated in Table 3.

Table 3: Breakdown of Soluble Nitrogen in Wheat and Barley Malts

	Barley malt	Wheat malt
High molecular weight	20%	40%
Middle molecular weight	20%	15%
Low molecular weight	60%	45%

The percentage of high-molecular-weight proteins in wheat is double that of barley, thus hindering a speedy lautering process and the clarification of the beer during cellaring. The low percentage of low-molecular-weight proteins in wheat malt translates to a low level of free amino nitrogen in the wort. This deficiency must be compensated for in the mash-tun to provide the yeast cells with these necessary building blocks. Because German malts are usually not as highly modified as British or American malts, it essential that an abundant supply of amino acids be secured by decoction mashing, and by resting the mash at the temperature optima of the proteolytic enzymes.

Typical mash-in temperatures are 95 to 99 degrees F (35 to 37 degrees C). These temperatures are used, even though they are below the optima of the key proteases, because they help to dissolve pre-existing soluble substances, which facilitates sufficient breakdown of wheat proteins. More importantly, the endo, amino and carboxy peptidases all demonstrate higher activity when a mash-in temperature of 95 degrees F (35 degrees C) is chosen over a mash-in temperature of 122 degrees F (50 degrees C).[83] After mash-in, the temperature is raised 1 degree C per minute until the desired protein rest temperature is reached. A lengthy protein rest must then be observed. To cover the differing temperature optima of the three enzyme groups, many breweries opt for a staggered protein rest—at 117, 122, and 126 degrees F (47, 50, and 52 degrees C), for example.

Decoction mashing is necessary not only to maximize the breakdown of proteins, but to attain the highest possible degree of starch breakdown as well. Proteolytic modification in the malthouse is the limiting factor in the production of wheat malt. If it is overdone, cytolytic modification will be up to par, but the negative aspects of high protein modification will come to the fore (decreased foam retention values and increased color).[84] A compromise must be made, and malt that is cytolytically undermodified is the result. This under-modification results in the relatively high viscosity of worts made with wheat malt. A decoction mash is best to reduce the undesired effects of this phenomenon, using heat to break down the viscous substances. The amylases can then more efficiently convert malt starch into wort sugars. Coarse grits that otherwise remain encased in a layer of glutinous substances are broken down into smaller particles, and starch conversion is more complete.

If enzyme-rich barley malt is being used, and the grist composition contains no more than 50 percent wheat malt, a step infusion mash is possible. The barley malt should be very well modified, and the degree of protein solubility in the wheat malt should be above 40 percent. Six-row barley malt helps to increase the amount of enzymes and amino acids in the wort. If an authentic Weissbier is desired, however, at least a single decoction mash should be employed. The number of breweries that use an infusion mash to brew Weissbier is extremely limited, and I personally know of none that use a single-step infusion mash.

A typical Weissbier will have an apparent degree of attenuation around 80 percent, which requires a maltose rest of moderate length and a low saccharification temperature. Maltose rests can be held for 10 to 30 minutes—less if a sweeter Weissbier is desired, more if a dry one is being brewed. The saccharification temperature of a Weissbier is almost invariably between 158 to 162 degrees F (70 to 72 degrees C).

The most intensive mash program commonly used for brewing a Weissbier is the double decoction mash. This mash program is chosen for malts that are not highly modified, particularly if the degree of soluble protein is less than 36 percent, or if the viscosity is unusually high (greater than 1.8 mPas). A double decoction mash is also well suited for brewing a Dunkles Weissbier or a Weizenbock. It not only develops the full-bodied character of these beers, but helps to increase the amino acid concentration of their worts, as darker malts typically yield less amino acids than pale malts. Boiling the decoction mash twice instead of once also helps to deepen the color and intensify the malty, breadlike aroma and flavor of a Dunkelweizen or Weizenbock.

Diagram 1 depicts the steps of a double decoction

Diagram 1: Double Decoction Mash for Weissbier

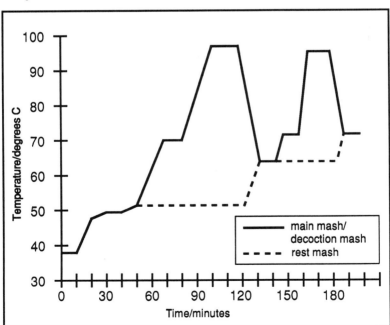

mashing process. The grains are mashed in at 99 degrees F (37 degrees C) with a water to grist ratio of 3 to 1 or 3.5 to 1. After the mash-in is completed the temperature of the mash is raised 1 degree C per minute up to 117 degrees F (47 degrees C). At this temperature the staggered protein rest begins, which will optimize protein breakdown. The mash temperature is slowly raised to 122 degrees F (50 degrees C), and at this temperature a short rest of 10 to 15 minutes is held. The mash temperature is raised over the course of 10 minutes to 127 degrees (53 degrees C). If the malt is very poorly modified, these times can all be extended by 20 to 30 percent to insure adequate protein breakdown.

The first decoction is thick, with a concentration of about 2 to 1. Its temperature is raised about 1 degree C per minute to 158 to 162 degrees F (70 to 72 degrees C), at which point a saccharification rest of 10 to 15 minutes is observed. In some cases a short maltose rest at 145 to 149 degrees F (63 to 65 degrees C) is also held before the saccharification temperature is reached. After the iodine reaction has proven negative the mash is brought to a boil in 15 to 20 minutes. The length of the boil should be less than 20 minutes; otherwise, the color of the wort will be too deep for a pale Hefe Weissbier. The decoction mash is added to the rest mash and a maltose rest of 10 to 15 minutes at 145 to 149 degrees F (63 to 65 degrees C) is held before the second decoction is pulled. This mash is thick, but not as concentrated as the first decoction (2.5 to 1). Again, a short saccharification rest is observed before the decoction mash is brought to a boil. This mash is boiled for the same length of time as the first decoction, or slightly less. The saccharification temperature after the two mashes have been combined is 158 to 162 degrees F (70 to 72 degrees C). Once the iodine test has proven negative the temperature of the mash is raised to the mash-off temperature of 169 to 172 degrees F (76 to 78 degrees C). The total duration of this mashing procedure is about three and a half hours.

Diagram 2: Single Decoction Mash for Weissbier

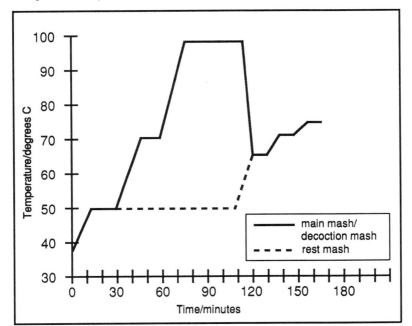

As the quality of malts has improved over the years, many breweries have found the double decoction mash to be superfluous, and have determined that a single decoction mash is sufficient to brew a classic Weissbier. More and more breweries are switching over to a single decoction mash for their Weissbiers in the interests of energy conservation and to save time in the brewhouse. Time is critical for those breweries that have a production bottleneck in the brewhouse.

Diagram 2 depicts a typical single decoction mash used to brew a Weissbier. The grains are mashed in at 99 degrees F (37 degrees C) and raised 1 degree C per minute to 122 degrees F (50 degrees C). At this temperature a protein rest of 20 minutes is held, then a thick decoction is pulled, and the temperature is raised 1 degree C per minute until the saccharification temperature of 158 to 162 degrees F (70 to 72 degrees C) is reached. The mash is allowed to rest at this temperature until a negative iodine reaction occurs (10 to 15 minutes). It is then heated to boiling in 10 minutes.

Because only one decoction is being pulled, it is necessary to extend the boiling time beyond that of a double decoction mash to at least 30 minutes, in some cases 40. The two mashes are combined slowly and the temperature of the whole is raised to 145 to 149 degrees F (63 to 65 degrees C) and held here for 10 to 20 minutes. The temperature is then raised again to the saccharification temperature of 158 to 162 degrees F (70 to 72 degrees C), at which the mash rests until the starch conversion end point is verified by the iodine test. The mash is then raised to the mash-off temperature of 169 degrees F (76 degrees C), is held here for

Diagram 3: Single Decoction Mash for Weissbier

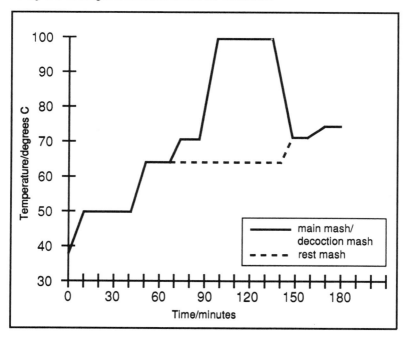

5 to 10 minutes, and then is transferred to the lauter-tun.

Another commonly used single decoction mash program (Diagram 3) subjects the entire mash to a protein rest before the decoction is pulled. Using infusions the temperature of the mash is raised from the mash-in temperature to the protein rest temperature and then again to the maltose rest temperature. The entire mash is subjected to the maltose rest temperature of 147 degrees F (64 degrees C) for 10 to 20 minutes before the thick decoction is pulled. It is then handled similarly to the decoction in the mash program in Diagram 2. This variation is suitable if the malt is proteolytically well modified and/or if a wort that is highly attenuable is being brewed.

Some variation of a decoction mash is common to virtually every Weissbier that is brewed in the Germanic world. Even if enzyme-strong malts are being used, the biochemical process of starch and protein decomposition is insufficient to reduce the troublesome higher molecular weight proteins and at the same time supply the wort with a sufficient amount of amino acids necessary for a speedy fermentation, optimal yeast reproduction and a minimum of undesirable fermentation byproducts (vicinal diketones, fusel alcohols). A decoction mash is also necessary to break down the cytolytically undermodified wheat malt to the point that starch conversion is complete so that the beer will not be plagued by starch haze. Physical/thermal energy is needed to reduce proteins and starch to levels that will preclude the problems associated with inadequate mashing of wheat malts.

LAUTERING

Once the mash program has been completed, lautering begins. The process varies among breweries. Some sparge continuously, others sparge periodically, at temperatures that vary between 167 and 174 degrees F (76 and 79 degrees C). Lautering a Weizen wort is sometimes tedious, because several factors work against an efficient runoff. Most obvious is the lack of husks in the mash. Wheat kernels do not have an outer husk, so the only source of husk material comes from the barley malt. Since the husks and coarse grits are essential for distancing grist particles from one another in the lauter mash, their diminished presence in wheat beer worts will impede the lautering process. Crushing the grain more coarsely would help to loosen the lauter mash, but malt that is ground too coarsely will result in poor mash saccharification and decreased yield, which in turn will lead to all the problems outlined in the previous section.

The second hindrance to efficient lautering is the increased viscosity of wheat malt worts. The following table helps to illuminate this problem:

Table 4: Average Viscosities of German Wheat and Barley Malts 1988 Harvest*

	Wheat malt[85]		Barley malt[86]	
	Region A	Region B	Summer barley	Winter barley
Viscosity, mPas	1.70	1.66	1.48	1.58

* The figures for Region A (Erbachshof) and Region B (Köferling) represent the average viscosities of the winter wheat malts from those regions. The figures for summer and winter barley malts are averages of many growing regions. In both cases the averages were not derived from one particular strain, but from a variety of seed types.

The average viscosity of the two wheat malts is 0.20 higher than the viscosity of the summer barley, and the

Everything clear? Brilliant wort flows from the faucets of a Lautergrant.

absolute levels of each are far higher than is acceptable. No matter how intensive a mash program is implemented, wheat beer worts tend to be more viscous than worts made exclusively from barley malts. The high viscosity of wheat malt worts is attributable mainly to the protein structure of the wheat, not the gums or glucanes as is the case with all barley malts.[87]

Finally, the structure of wheat proteins is the source of another potential runoff problem. Excessive oxygen uptake in the mash will oxidize the sulfhydryl groups of proteins, causing disulfide bridges to form between proteins. Each bridge unites two smaller proteins into one larger one, thus increasing the amount of high-molecular-weight proteins, which is already higher than desired in a wheat malt wort. A slow, inefficient runoff is the result.

The modern Weissbier brewer combats these runoff problems in a number of ways. To keep the barley husks intact, the barley malt is crushed as gently as possible. It is easier to retain intact barley husks if the malt is conditioned

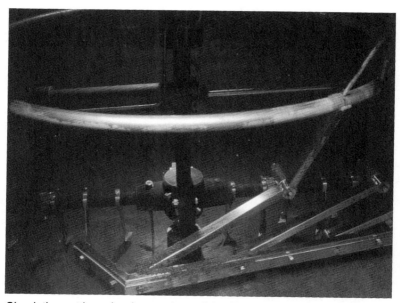

Circulating cutting rakes loosen the grainbed in the lauter tun so that the wort can flow to the brew kettle.

or wet milled. Mashing and lautering with minimal oxygen uptake will prevent the oxidation of proteins, and thus reduce the chances of a sluggish or set lauter mash. Timely use of the cutting machine reduces the resistance of the grain bed to the runoff wort. Some breweries run the cutting jack continuously. Reducing the load of the grain in the lauter-tun is also effective; because wheat mashes are more tightly packed, a set mash may result if the load on the false bottom exceeds 200 kg/m². Underletting the mash with water may also help. Ultimately, the brewer can minimize headaches in the brewhouse by selecting malts that are easy to work with, and by minimizing oxygen uptake during the mash. Well-modified, low-protein and low-viscosity malts will benefit the lautering process and produce a Weissbier wort that meets the highest standards of quantity and quality.

BOILING A WEIZEN WORT

A wheat beer wort is boiled in much the same manner as an all-barley-malt wort, with two exceptions. Malt is emphasized over hops in Weissbier, and hopping rates seldom exceed 18 IBU. Because the hop plays second fiddle to the grain in German style wheat beers, the variety of the hops used is not crucial. Bittering hops are most commonly used in Weissbiers, but lower grade aroma hops can also be used to improve the quality of the hop bitterness. Due to their high level of coagulable protein, Weissbier worts must be boiled longer than normal. The reduced level of hop tannins, which aid the coagulation of wort proteins, also necessitates a longer boil. A typical boil time is one and a half to two hours and, if an extremely high proportion of wheat malt is used, the boiling time can be even longer. If a system with an external boiler is being used, then a boiling time of 70 to 80 minutes at 226 to 230 degrees F (108 to 110 degrees C) is sufficient. To minimize the chances of chill haze in the packaged beer, the amount of coagulable protein should be reduced to less than 3 mg/100 mL.

Once the boil has been completed, the wort is usually whirpooled to remove the hot trub from it. However, many breweries opt to centrifuge the wort prior to cooling it. If hot trub separation is insufficient, the resulting Weissbier tastes astringently bitter. Cold trub separation is another matter, and many breweries choose not to separate the cold trub from the Weissbier wort. However, because wheat beer worts produce a higher concentration of cold trub than barley worts,[88] separating this trub fraction to some degree may be desirable. The typical procedures for a cold trub separation are cold sedimentation and flotation.

5

Fermenting, Conditioning and Packaging Weissbier

All German wheat beers are fermented with *Saccharo-myces cerevisiae*, or top-fermenting yeasts, which are typically harvested from the surface of the green beer. According to the German Beer Tax Law (Biersteuergesetz), which is known more loosely as the Reinheitsgebot, only malted barley may be used for bottom-fermented beers. Thus, it is forbidden to make a lager wheat beer in Germany. Typical pitching rates range from 1/4 to 1/2 L of thick, pasty yeast per hL of cast-out wort. If a more precise means of yeast pitching is used, then 10 to 15 million cells per mL of wort are dosed. In the classic Weissbier brewery, open vat fermentations are the rule, and the yeast is either scooped off with a slotted spoon or cropped off with a skimmer, or it runs over into a collecting trough. Wheat beer yeasts from open fermentations are often used hundreds of times without a loss of vitality. Though the larger breweries have switched to closed fermentations, many swear open fermented Weissbiers taste better than those fermented in cylindro-conical tanks. If a closed fermentation is used, the yeast can only be repitched five to 10 times before it loses its vitality.

The characteristic flavors of Weizen beers are produced

only by those yeast strains that have traditionally been used for Weissbier fermentation. To attempt to brew a classic Weissbier using English ale yeast would be like trying to make a single-malt scotch in Japan. The result is simply untrue to the style. At the end of the 1970s one of the great secrets of Bavarian-style wheat beers was unlocked when it was discovered that 4-vinyl guaiacol was largely responsible for their typical phenolic flavor. The precursor to 4-vinyl guaiacol, ferulic acid, is present in Weissbier worts in amounts ranging from 3 to 5 ppm. During fermentation the yeast takes up the ferulic acid and decarboxylizes it to 4-vinyl guaiacol.[89] However, it can do this only when ferulic acid is present in its free form.[90] Normally, ferulic acid is bound to the pentosanes in grains with ester bonds.[91] These bonds are broken during mashing, most effectively at temperatures of 111 degrees F (44 degrees C) and at a pH of 5.7.[92]

Of all of the yeast strains thus far tested, only a few have been able to convert ferulic acid into this leading aroma and flavor substance in Weizen beer.[93] One of these yeast strains is found in the majority of wheat beer breweries of Southern Germany. The culture yeast is not the only microorganism capable of converting the phenol carbonic acids to phenols; infections of wild yeast, wort bacteria and lactic acid bacteria also can raise the concentration of the phenols.[94]

Weissbier can be fermented at warmer or colder temperatures. If the temperature dips below 54 degrees F (12 degrees C), the fermentation will be sluggish, and if it rises above 77 degrees F (25 degrees C) the beer becomes increasingly infection-prone and will be plagued with high concentrations of esters and fusel alcohols. These aroma and flavor components, however, are a characteristic part of a Weissbier profile, so brewers try to create a balance among them by fermenting the beer at temperatures between these two extremes. There is an old rule of thumb among Weissbier brewers that the sum of the pitching and the fermentation temperatures should equal 30 degrees C for a Weissbier of superior quality to result. Most breweries adhere to this rule. A very common procedure is to pitch the yeast at 54 degrees F (12 degrees C), and ferment at 64 degrees F (18 degrees C). If a brewer wishes to use a colder fermentation of 55 to 59 degrees F (13 to 15 degrees C), the yeast is pitched at 63 degrees F (17 degrees C).

After 12 hours, the so-called hop drive takes place, in which the rising yeast carries hop resins and trub particles to the surface of the fermentation. If the beer is fermenting in open vessels, these particles can be removed using a slotted spoon or scraper. This practice is done within the next 24 hours to ensure a clean fermentation and to minimize the amount of unwanted substances in the harvest yeast. When the beer demonstrates a kraeusenlike character after 24 to 36 hours, the yeast is harvested from the surface of the fermenting beer. Slow or incomplete rising of the yeast usually indicates a weak yeast, although cold fermentation tem-

A brewer prepares to crop yeast from an open fermenter. The traditional method of skimming Weissbier yeast from the surface of the fermenting beer is still widely practiced in Germany.

In this brewery, the beer is still handmade: trub is separated from Weissbier wort with a "trubsack."

peratures, insufficient wort aeration or poor wort composition (e.g., an amino acid deficit or misproportion of fermentable sugars) also can be factors. Sluggish rising of the yeast ultimately results in off-flavors in the beer. The primary fermentation is usually complete after 72 hours.

After the young beer reaches final gravity, it can be handled in a variety of ways. Many brewers choose to lager the beer between five and 28 days at cooler temperatures before it is primed and bottled. The beer will be clearer, particularly at lower temperatures, if it is allowed to settle in an intermediary holding tank. In Germany isinglass may be used to aid the clarification of top-fermenting beers, but only in such a conditioning tank. It may not be used to clarify the beer once it has been packaged; i.e., used for bottle conditioning. This settling period will also benefit the bouquet and flavor of the beer because it is still slightly active and unwanted volatile substances can be driven from it. The cooler the temperature, the better. Best results are obtained when the temperature in the conditioning tank is between 39 and 46 degrees F (4 and 8 degrees C).

Weissbier brewed in the classic fashion is allowed to ferment to the point of terminal gravity, and then is primed and bottle conditioned. To obtain the desired CO_2 concentration and mature flavor and aroma in the bottled beer, a predetermined amount of Speise is mixed with the young beer just prior to bottling. This procedure is much simpler than allowing the beer to ferment until a precalculated amount of residual extract remains in solution for carbonation purposes. Given how fast a Weissbier can ferment, the desired degree of fermentation may be reached in the middle of the night when bottling is impossible.

Many breweries filter the young beer prior to adding the Spiese. Filtering is essential if the beer has not been held in a storage/conditioning tank after the primary fermentation, or if the settling/conditioning time has been short. Even though some yeast is necessary for bottle conditioning, if the yeast cell count is too high the finished beer will be cloudy and will have an undesirable, yeasty-bitter taste. Although many breweries centrifuge the young beer to reduce the yeast count, filtration is an attractive option because it removes all the yeast from the young beer. The amount of yeast needed for bottle conditioning then can be dosed exactly, thus enabling the brewmaster to more precisely define and monitor the course of the secondary fermentation. Another benefit of completely removing the top-fermenting yeast from the young beer is that the brewery can have only lager yeast in the bottle for conditioning. The advantages of using bottom-fermenting yeast to bottle condition Weissbier will be seen shortly.

Even if the young beer is to be filtered, preclarifying the beer in a settling or conditioning tank is desirable. The fewer yeast cells in the beer, the less particulate matter there is to clog the filter, which allows the filtration process to run longer before the pressure build-up brings it to a halt. In fact, the clarification process in the tank may make later filtration unneccessary. Most breweries that do not use a conditioning tank at least hold the beer for a few days in a settling tank to allow some preclarification of the beer, which saves on filtration costs. Horizontal tanks work much better than vertical ones as settling/conditioning tanks. Often the Speise is filtered along with the young beer to remove the coagulable proteins present in the Speise. Because of the increased number of higher molecular weight proteins in the young beer, filtration problems are often encountered even if the flocculation and sedimentation of the yeast has been sufficient.

The Speise, the young beer and any yeast added for bottle conditioning must be mixed thoroughly so that all bottles contain the three elements in equal proportions. The Speise, young beer and yeast can be mixed in a tank with some kind of mixing unit in it, or the Speise can be dosed into the pipeline leading to the bottler. The small Weissbier brewery where I worked in 1987 had just recently begun using its custom-built mixing tank. Prior to that, the mixing device consisted of a large, open tank, two mixing paddles, and a couple of cranky beer drivers who did not appreciate being called away from their deliveries to hand mix 60 hL of beer!

A common and relatively inexpensive method of mixing the three elements is to use a pump that recirculates the mixture in the tank. When designing such a tank, it is important to position the inlet from the pressure side of the pump low in the tank. If the inlet is above the surface of the beer, excessive foaming will take place. The inlet also should be positioned as far away from the tank outlet as possible, which can be accomplished much more effectively in a horizontal tank. The worst possible design for such a mixing tank would be some type of cylindro-conical tank. Because the inlet must be low, it would feed right into the outlet at the bottom of the cone, and the contents at the top of the tank would not be mixed. Angling the inlet upward 25 to 40 degrees will send the incoming mixture in an upward direction, helping to distribute it more evenly in the tank. It is important to circulate the contents of the tank for 30 minutes or so prior to bottling, particularly if the Speise and the young beer have been in the tank for more than a few hours.

Another common and inexpensive means of mixing the Speise, young beer and yeast is to equip the mixing tank with a rotating mixing paddle. To prevent foaming, the paddle must be placed low in the tank, and the rotation speed must be reduced when the surface of the liquid has sunk below the top of the paddle arms. Mixing tanks equipped with a paddle can be vertical, even cylindro-conical tanks. The blades of the paddle should be twisted like the blades of a fan or propellor so that they will drive the liquid in an upward direction. If the blades are designed in this way, the mixing will be more thorough at a lower speed, thus maximizing homogeneity while having minimal impact on the beer and yeast cells. In any case, speeds greater than 40 rpm should be avoided.

A more sophisticated method of ensuring that the proper amounts of Speise and yeast are added to the young beer is to dose both of them directly into the feed line of the bottler. Most commonly the yeast is dosed into the feed line, while the Speise and young beer are still combined in a mixing tank. The advantage of this system is that an exact amount of yeast can be dosed into the feed line directly from a propagation tank.

The amount of Speise added to the young beer depends on the desired degree of carbonation, the gravity of the young beer and the starting and final gravities of the Speise. Based on Balling's studies of fermentation, 1 g of fermentable extract yields 0.46 g CO_2. Beer at atmospheric pressure contains approximately 0.2 percent, or 2 g/L, of CO_2. If the desired CO_2 content of the packaged beer is 0.7 percent by weight (a typical amount for Weissbier), then 1.08 g extract must be added to the beer, which will result in the development of 0.5 g/L of CO_2 when it ferments in the bottle. If the starting and real final gravities of the Speise are known, then the amount of Speise (relative to the amount of young beer) that needs to be added to the young beer can be calculated using the following formula:

$$\% \text{ Speise} = \frac{\dfrac{\% \text{ desired } CO_2 \text{ content} - 0.2}{0.46}}{\text{starting gravity} - \text{real final gravity (°Plato)}} \times 100$$

The resulting mixture is usually 1.0 to 1.5 °Plato higher than the extract of the young beer. It is necessary to know the final gravity of the Speise wort in order to make this calculation, but this can be determined in a matter of hours with a rapid fermenting yeast that is pitched in excess to a wort sample. The real terminal limit of attenuation can be determined by multiplying the apparent terminal limit of attenuation by 0.81. The real final gravity can then be determined through substitution:

(1) apparent terminal limit of attenuation (ATLA)
$$= \frac{\text{OG} - \text{apparent terminal gravity}}{\text{OG}}$$

(2) real terminal limit of attenuation (RTLA) = ATLA x 0.81
$$= \frac{\text{OG} - \text{real final gravity}}{\text{OG}}$$

(3) real terminal gravity = OG(1 - RTLA)

Note: Degrees and limits of attenuation are commonly expressed in percent, but to simplify this example the equations have been written to express the limits of attenuation in decimal fractions less than 1. Multiply equations (1) and (2) by 100 to express the degree of attenuation in percent.

The Speise itself can be the first runnings of the lauter wort, or boiled and hopped kettle wort. If first runnings are used, it is necessary to sterilize them and, if kettle wort is used, caution must be taken to use a wort that is not excessively hopped. If, for example, the Speise had 40 BU, the young beer had 12 BU, and a Speise volume equal to 13 percent of the young beer must be added to reach the desired level of carbonation, the BU of the total mixture would increase to 15.6.

If the remaining yeast cells have been removed from the young beer by filtration, enough yeast must be added to the young-beer/Speise mixture to ensure a secondary fermentation in the bottle or keg. Approximately 2 to 4 milliliters of top-fermenting yeast is added to each liter of Speise and young beer (or one-quarter to one-half ounce per gallon), slightly more if a Weizenbock is being brewed.[95] This formula translates to about 1 liter of thick yeast paste per hectoliter of Speise that is being used. The yeast is added just prior to bottling to minimize the fermentation that takes place before the beer is bottled. Although top-fermenting yeast is used to ferment a Weissbier, either top- or bottom-fermenting yeast can be added to the young-beer/ Speise mixture for the bottle conditioning. Some breweries choose to use lager yeast for the secondary fermentation because it generally sediments and flocculates better than ale yeast, thus clarifying the beer better. The German beer tax law recognizes this fact, but limits the amount of lager yeast that can be added to the young beer to 0.1 percent of

Meticulously cleaned and very modern—the fermentation and storage cellar at the Erdinger Weissbier Brewery.

the amount of wort that was pitched with top-fermenting yeast. Thus, breweries that use lager yeast for the bottle conditioning are limited to dosing only slightly more than 1 mL of bottom-fermenting yeast per liter of young beer. This amount is small enough to ensure that the wheat beer will retain its top-fermented character, but is sufficient to ferment the Speise that has been added to the young beer.

It is often easy to tell which breweries use lager yeast for the bottle conditioning, as these beers will have chunks of flocculated yeast floating in them. Beers conditioned with top-fermenting yeast or non-flocculating lager yeast will exhibit a veil-like haze as the yeast slowly sifts to the bottom of the glass. Top-fermenting yeast also tends to autolyze quicker than bottom-fermenting yeast, and so affects the flavor stability of Weissbiers that are distributed over a large area or stored for long periods of time. Despite the technological and cosmetic benefits of using lager yeast for the conditioning process, many of the more traditional Weissbier breweries insist upon the exclusive use of top-fermenting yeast for both the primary and the bottle fermentations.

Instead of adding yeast to the Speise and the filtered or

unfiltered young beer, some breweries use bottom-ferment-ing kraeusen beer as a primer for the bottles. Using kraeusen has two advantages. First, the secondary fermentation begins immediately after the kraeusen is added to the young beer. If yeast is added to Speise and filtered young beer, it must first adapt to the substrate and overcome the lag phase before the secondary fermentation begins. Second, bottle fermentation is effective at lower temperatures, eliminating the need for the warm phase of the bottle conditioning (see page 83). When brewers use kraeusen, they mix it with the young beer and bottle as soon as possible after the gravity has been determined, due to the rapid attenuation that takes place during high kraeusen.

German Weissbier brewers must make sure that the amount of bottom-fermenting kraeusen added to the young beer does not exceed the maximum allowable amount specified by the German beer tax law (Biersteuergesetz) which is 15 percent of the amount of wort that was pitched with top-fermenting yeast. Brewers are also careful to make sure that the addition of bottom-fermenting kraeusen beer does not reduce the percentage of wheat in the beer to below 50 percent. (Consumers expect a Weissbier to contain at least that amount of wheat, though it is not a legal require-ment.) If a brewer uses a grist ratio of 51 to 49 malted wheat to malted barley, then adds 15 percent bottom-fermented kraeusen beer (which, according to the beer tax law, has been made with 100 percent malted barley) to the young Weissbier, the ratio of malted wheat that has been used to make the finished beer is less than 50 percent.

The young-beer/Speise mixture is extremely turbid at the time of bottling. The conditioning period after packaging serves not only to clarify the beer, but to carbonate the beer as well. Weissbier is probably the easiest beer to bottle in a German brewery. Because the CO_2 content of the beer will be established

Clip-on manometers are placed on the bottles to monitor the pressure build-up during the bottle fermentation. Once the desired pressure has been reached, the cold phase of the bottle conditioning begins.

during the conditioning phase, the young-beer/Speise mixture can be bottled at atmospheric pressure (depending on the bottler being used), thus eliminating the need for counter-pressure bottling. It is not necessary to use a sophisticated bottler that pre-evacuates the bottle, because the yeast will take up any air that is taken up at the bottling stage during the bottle fermentation. Nevertheless, excessive oxygen uptake should be avoided. Care must be taken that the biological conditions at the time of packaging are absolutely sterile. There is a plethora of available nutrients in the form of unfermented extract in the bottle, and because the initial phase of the secondary fermentation takes place at high temperatures, just one lactic acid bacterium can wreak havoc on the character of the beer.[96] Weissbier is almost always bottled into half-liter brown bottles that are sealed with crown caps.

The Weissbier at this point is quite flat and, particularly if the Speise is kettle wort, rather worty tasting. My co-workers at Brauerei Widmann told me of the laxative quality of the young-beer/Speise mixture after I had complained of irregularity. This ancient Bavarian remedy actually seemed to work. Once the beer has been bottled and put into cases, it is moved into what the Germans call "Boxen," giant rooms that are equipped with both heaters and cooling units. Some breweries have separate boxes for the warm and cold phases of the bottle conditioning. The beer is brought into the boxes by hand or forklift, depending on the size of the brewery, and is left to sit at approximately 68 degrees F (20 degrees C) for two to five days until the CO_2 has built up to the desired level. Subjecting the bottles to warm temperatures, which in some breweries exceed 77 degrees F (25 degrees C), jump starts the secondary fermentation so that most of the remaining extract is fermented within three to four days. The effectiveness of this rapid bottle fermentation is measured with clip-on manometers that measure the head pressure in a few sample bottles. When the registered pressure corresponds with the pressure the brewmaster has calculated should be present, or after the pressure has not increased over one full day, the cooling system in the uni-box is turned on, or the beer is transferred from the warm box to the cold box. The cold storage should last for at least two weeks and can be as long as six, particularly if the beer is a Weizenbock. During this time the beer matures and clarifies before it leaves the brewery bound for a restaurant or Biergarten.

A recent innovation in the packaging of Hefe Weissbier has been the implementation of kegs. The principle is the same as bottling Weissbier: a young beer, Speise and yeast mixture is packaged in the keg, and the secondary fermentation is carried out until manometers placed on sample kegs register the pre-calculated pressure. The difficulty with kegged Weissbier is tapping the keg for dispensing. Because the CO_2 content of Weissbier is relatively high and greater-than-normal feed pressures are necessary to pump the beer from the keg into the glass, problems can arise, particularly if there is a significant height difference between the storage cooler and the tap. Obviously, beer lines and tap heads must be cooled to avoid excessive foaming while pouring.

6

How To Drink a Weissbier and What To Eat With It

Weissbier is almost always drunk from a glass. It is so highly carbonated that attempting to drink it from a bottle will leave the drinker with little more than a mouthful of foam. I don't mean that I have never seen Weissbier being drunk directly from the bottle, but it is uncommon, and a beer that is so complex should be enjoyed in the appropriate container to appreciate the full depth of its flavor and aroma.

One of the most striking characteristics of a Weissbier is the peculiarly shaped glass that it is served in. The reason for its shape has long been a subject of debate among brewers, some arguing that it allows for easier pouring, others contending that it helps the foam stability of the beer. Some Weissbier glasses have a rough bottom, thus facilitating a greater release of carbon dioxide from the beer. There are many variations on the theme of the Weissbier glass, but all have a vase shape with a narrow base and a wide mouth.

One of the greatest challenges a Weissbier drinker faces is getting the beer from the bottle into the glass. Because of the high CO_2 concentration of Weissbier, it foams excessively unless it is carefully and slowly poured into the glass.

A fine example of the master pour.

If a Weissbier drinker attempts to pour the Weissbier violently, at best a quarter of the contents of the bottle will make it into the glass. The rest will overflow, and what is left in the glass will require a settling time of half an hour before the sip or two of beer can be drunk without getting a mouthful of foam. Therefore, it is important to follow the steps in one of the two methods described below to avoid complete embarassment when pouring Weissbier.

METHOD 1: FLASHY NIGHTCLUB BARTENDER'S POUR

Place the Weissbier glass upside down on top of the bottle. The glass should go about halfway down the bottle before it is stopped. Quickly turn the glass and bottle over so the glass is now right side up and the bottle is upside down. The beer will rapidly pour out of the bottle until the mouth of the bottle is submerged. Then slowly pull the bottle out of the glass, keeping the mouth of the bottle beneath the surface of the beer until the bottle is empty. It is important that the mouth of the bottle stay beneath the surface of the beer, not just the foam, otherwise the beer will foam over out of the glass. This method is commonly found in chic nightclubs or gastronomical institutions where bartenders are feverishly pouring Weissbier. It is *not* the method I recommend, because it is unsanitary. Though the inside of the bottle is perfectly clean, the exterior of the bottle may be dirtied with dust, detergent or glue residues.

METHOD 2: THE MASTER POUR

This method should always be used when pouring fine quality Weissbier. Hold the bottle in the dominant hand and the glass in the other hand. Tip the bottle as far as possible without letting any beer flow out, then tip the glass slightly downward and bring it over the mouth of the tilted bottle. Now slowly tilt the glass upright and begin decanting the beer *slowly* down the side of the glass with the mouth of the bottle as far down the glass as possible, without ever letting it come in contact with the beer or foam. When done properly, there should be little foam on the surface of the beer. Once the glass is almost full, the bottle can be raised a couple of inches from the rim and the remaining beer can be poured more vigorously to raise the head.

Of course, both of these methods will fail if the glass is not completely clean and free of dust prior to pouring. If there is dust in the glass, there will be a massive release of

CO_2, causing excessive foaming, and if the glass is greasy or tainted with detergent residues, the head will be small and unstable. To help prevent over-foaming when pouring, it is customary to rinse the glass with cold water first. The best serving temperature for Weissbier is between 46 and 50 degrees F (8 and 10 degrees C).

Weissbier is not just Weissbier, it is Hefe Weissbier. Some like to get every last yeast cell from the bottle to the glass, while others try to decant the beer off the yeast sediment so that little or no yeast is in the glass. Most prefer it *Mit Hefe* (with yeast), and there are a variety of ways to make sure that the yeast gets from the bottle to the glass. When pouring a Weissbier that is meant to have yeast in it, empty the bottle down to the last half inch of beer. Then gently shake the bottle or use a circular movement to loosen the yeast sediment from the bottom of the bottle. At this point the remaining contents can be emptied into the glass. This method is not good enough for some, because it does not extract every last yeast cell from the bottle. It is not uncommon to see these people violently shaking their bottles, or even rolling them back and forth across a table. Such procedures lead to violent foaming of the remaining beer in the bottle. By the time this foam has settled, those who have used a gentler means of loosening the yeast sediment will already be on their second beer. But this concern with the yeast is just another one of the gimmicks associated with this unique beer, and if some want to make a game out of pouring it, more power to them.

One of the most controversial gimmicks associated with Weissbier is adding a lemon slice to the glass. This tradition was not inspired by the marketing tactics of certain Latin American breweries, but no one knows for sure where it came from. It is quite common to add a lemon slice to Kristall Weizen, particularly in Austria, but if you shuffle up to the bar in Bavaria and ask for a lemon slice in your Hefe Weissbier, the place will become deathly silent. You will definitely get some mean looks from the other pub goers and the bartender will curse at you under his breath or even directly at you. Really, this is quite understandable. Would you drink a 20-year-old single-malt scotch whisky on the rocks? Would you put steak sauce on a tender filet? Weissbier undergoes one of the most painstaking brewing processes of any beer. The master brewer who has laboriously toiled to make a fine quality Weissbier shudders to think that anyone would want to mask the natural flavor of the beer by adding a lemon slice to it. What's more, it just isn't natural. I never once saw a lemon tree the whole time I was in Germany.

Unfortunately, not too long ago in Germany a few heretics banded together and decided to dilute the taste of the world's finest beers by mixing them with soda pop. Yes, that's correct, soda pop. Apparently the trend was started when a group of bicyclists couldn't stand the heat on a summer's day and stopped at a Biergarten for refreshment. Some wiseacre got the idea to mix lager beer and *Limonade*, the German version of lemon-lime flavor soda pop, in a ratio of 1 to 1. The so-called "Radlermaß," or "bicyclists tankard," was born. Germans have never been short on ingenuity or creativity, so it was only a matter of time before the Weissbier version of the Radlermaß was conceived, called the "Rußmaß." If you visit a Biergarten in Bavaria, do not make the mistake of being the tourist-who-will-try-anything-in-a-foreign-country and ask for one of these two soda pop beers, or you may be disappointed.

Once the Weissbier is in the glass, it is time to enjoy it. Germans love to toast, so if you want to do as the Romans do, there are a couple of things to bear in mind. Proper Weissbier etiquette dictates that the bases of the glasses be struck, not the sides or mouths. This practice reduces the

Once the Weissbier has been successfully poured into a glass it's time to enjoy. Prost!

risk of breakage. After the toast, it is then important to strike the base of the glass on the table. This act signifies that you are only taking a sip, not swilling down the entire beer in three gulps. One of the funniest Weissbier stories I know involved a Japanese student colleague of mine at Weihenstephan. Several dozen students were gathered together and a toast was made. Masayuki proceeded to drain his entire beer, while the rest had just taken a sip. In Japan, touching the glass to the table after the toast means bottoms up!

Weissbier complements just about any type of food. In Germany, as I said earlier, it is part of the classic trio that includes Weisswurst and Brezen. It goes well with just about any meat-and-potatoes meal, including some of the classic Bavarian meals such as pork roast, potato dumpling and blue kraut, or the ever popular leg of pork. Weissbier is excellent with spicy food like Serbian or Turkish, the cultures of which are both strongly represented in Germany. Pale Weissbier goes well with lighter meals as well, such as salads or cheese-and-meat platters. Weissbier is excellent with Italian food, Tex-Mex and Oriental cuisine. There is not much that Weissbier does not complement, and that helps explain its ubiquitous presence in the restaurants, bars and nightclubs all over Southern Germany.

Now that the food is on the table and the Weissbier is in hand, it is time to take a sip. First, smell the fruity, spicy aroma of the beer. Roll a small sip onto the tongue and allow it to effervesce. Your mouth should almost explode as the smooth Weissbier fills it. The aftertaste should also be smooth, with only a slight hint of bitterness. Now smell it again and take a bigger sip, this time noticing the myriad flavors in the beer. You probably won't have identified them all by the time the glass is empty, but that's OK, because if you've planned ahead, you've got a couple more bottles in the fridge. Prost!

7

Recipes for the
Weizen Lover

The actual process of brewing a Weissbier is not particularly complicated, but obtaining certain raw materials outside of Germany may be difficult. Finding a supply of malted wheat is possible, but coming up with a true Weissbier yeast is not an easy task. There are many North American breweries that make wheat beers and there are currently several that make Weissbier. Unfortunately, only a select few of these beers are true to style, and quite often the problem stems from the yeast culture that has been used. As was mentioned earlier, the number of yeast strains capable of yielding the typically phenolic aroma and flavor of German Weissbiers is very small, and one strain in particular is used by the majority of the wheat beer breweries in Southern Germany. If a Berliner Weisse is going to be brewed, the appropriate yeast culture will be even more difficult to obtain, because few breweries produce this beer, and because the culture is not purely yeast, but also lactic acid bacteria.

To obtain the best results only a true Weissbier or Berliner Weisse culture should be used. Fine beers may result if other yeast cultures are employed, but the results will not be true to style. Finding dry Weissbier yeast is next to impossible, so in most cases a liquid culture must be used. The simplest way to procure the proper culture is to utilize the services of a yeast lab. Many American yeast labs have Weissbier yeasts for less than $100. Quality may vary with the lab, and you will have to specify that you want a German wheat beer yeast. For total security, a Weissbier yeast culture can be obtained from a Weissbier brewery in Germany or can be purchased from a German yeast bank. The price is significantly higher in this case, but at $200 a culture you will definitely get what you pay for. To investigate possible yeast sources see Appendix 2.

There is one other method of obtaining a Weissbier yeast that can be less expensive. It is definitely more time consuming, but it may be the best way to make a Weissbier that both is true to style and fits the particular flavor profile you want. If a particular Weissbier tastes fantastic to you, buy a bottle of it and perform a single-cell yeast culture yourself. If you possess neither the necessary equipment or the microbiological expertise, you may be able to have a lab or university culture the yeast for you. With this culture you may be able to brew a Weizen that possesses some of the flavor characteristics of the original beer. Of course, this procedure has its limitations. If the Weissbier you like has been filtered and dosed with lager yeast for the bottle conditioning, you are out of luck. About the only way to determine the yeast type is to view a sample of the yeast sediment under a microscope. This procedure will have to be done anyway in order to perform the single-cell culturing. If the bottle of Weissbier has been out of the brewery for a long time, many of the yeast cells may have autolyzed or mutated, so a number of single-cell cultures will have to be made and tested for vitality and performance. And, of course, Hefe Weissbiers that are imported to the United

States are often pasteurized, so the bottle of beer used for culturing may have to be sent directly from Germany or procured on a visit.

When actually preparing the Weissbier wort, there are a few things to bear in mind so the brewing process will run smoothly and the resulting beer will be of the highest quality. The quality of the brewing water in terms of hardness and alkalinity is not as important in brewing a Weissbier as in brewing a lager, but if the pH of the mash and kettle wort is at an optimum, the protein coagulation will be better and the possibility of chill haze greatly reduced. Adding gypsum or calcium chloride is helpful here. A biological mash acidification can also be carried out to lower the mash and kettle wort pH.

When crushing the malt it is particularly important that the barley be milled as gently as possible to preserve the husks. This factor becomes increasingly important as the percentage of wheat is increased in the grist. The wheat can be milled finer, but should not be pulverized. Most microbrewers use a two-roller mill. For best results with barley malt, the rollers should be gapped at 0.035 inches (0.9 mm) and operated at a speed of 15 kg/hour/cm of roller width. When the wheat malt is milled, the distance between the rollers can be decreased to 0.024 inches (0.6 mm) and the speed increased to 20 kg/hour/cm of roller width, or higher. Naturally, these settings are dependent upon the quality of the malts, and if the malt is undermodified, the milling speed should be reduced. If a two-roller mill is being used both malts should be well modified so that the best possible grist is yielded.

A mash-in temperature of 99 degrees F (37 degrees C) works best to help bring the enzymes into solution and thereby facilitate maximal protein breakdown during the period of protease activity. A higher mash-in temperature of

122 degrees F (50 degrees C) will result in less protease enzyme activity,[97] and only a true kamikaze would mash in at temperatures higher than 131 degrees F (55 degrees C) when using 50 percent or more wheat malt in the grist.

It is not advisable to use an infusion mash program for the production of Weissbiers containing high percentages of wheat. At least a single decoction mash should be used and, if a Dunkles Weizen or Weizenbock is being brewed, then use a double decoction mash. If a microbrewery is not capable of decoction mashing, then it is imperative that enzyme-strong, well modified malts be used. The problem here is that such malts are often higher in protein content then malts of lower enzymatic power. Although six-row malts are extremely enzyme rich, they have a protein content that is higher than ideal for making a Weissbier. If there is no alternative other than to use an infusion mash, then use a step infusion mash that emphasizes the protease and amylase temperature optima.

When lautering remember that wheat beer mashes are more likely to set than all-barley malt mashes. Aside from properly milling and mashing the grains, reducing the load on the false bottom may improve the lautering performance. It is also wise to lauter more slowly when brewing Weissbier. Particularly at the beginning of lautering, flow rates should be low to avoid setting the mash.

Boiling time should be at least one and a half hours to obtain maximal protein coagulation, and the boil hops should be added as soon as the wort comes to a boil. Although not in accordance with the Reinheitsgebot, using some type of protein coagulant in the boil, such as Irish moss, may help to maximize protein coagulation. A kettle pH that is as close as possible to 5.2 will optimize this process as well.

Once the hot trub has been removed, the wort should

be cooled rapidly. Although some breweries choose to remove the cold trub to some degree or another, this really is not essential, particularly because the beer is racked at least once, often twice, from the sedimented matter. Pitching rates should be about one-third to one-half quart per barrel or, more exactly, 10 to 15 million cells per mL of wort. If a Weizenbock is being brewed this rate should be increased by 30 to 50 percent. I recommend pitching at about 59 degrees F (15 degrees C), but temperatures as high as 68 degrees F (20 degrees C) are acceptable.

The fermentation parameters greatly influence the character of the finished beer, so manipulating the fermentation variables will produce vastly differing beers. If a "clean" Weissbier that is low in phenols, esters and higher alcohols is desired, a lower gravity wort should be brewed, the fermentation temperature should be low, closed fermenters should be used and aeration levels should be normal or slightly increased. If phenols and esters are desired, then the exact opposite should be done, but for reasons of microbiological security and to keep the higher alcohols to a non-stupifying level, fermentation temperatures of 72 degrees F (22 degrees C) should not be exceeded. It is probably best to let the Weissbier ferment to the point of end attenuation and then add the Speise to it prior to bottle conditioning. Coordinating the bottling of the Weissbier with the necessary amount of residual extract still in it can be a tricky matter of timing, particularly if the beer is ready to be bottled in the middle of the night.

For most homebrewers it is not easy to filter the beer, so subjecting the young beer to a period of cold conditioning prior to bottling will help to clarify it. This should be done for three to seven days at temperatures of 39 to 45 degrees F (4 to 7 degrees C). Microbrewers may want to filter the young beer before adding the Speise, particularly if they are using a lager yeast for the bottle conditioning. Homebrewers who do not brew very often can save some of the cast-out wort for the bottling the following week. A quart and a half of Speise is usually sufficient for a 5-gallon batch of Weissbier of standard gravity, slightly less if the Speise has a high gravity or if the Weissbier is not intended to be overly carbonated. In most cases enough Speise extract will have to be added to the young beer to raise the gravity of the mixture by 1.004 to 1.006 (1.0 to 1.5 °Plato), depending on the desired degree of carbonation. This amount usually corresponds to about 9 to 13 percent of the amount of young beer, if cast-out wort is being used. It is always best to calculate the necessary amount of extract to obtain the most precise results. It works well to put hot cast-out wort into thick glass bottles and seal them with crown corks. Filling the bottles with hot wort virtually eliminates the possibility of an infection developing in them. Store them in a refrigerator until it is time to bottle.

Microbrewers or homebrewers who brew regularly can use cast out wort as Speise and add it to the young beer just prior to bottling. Of course, this means that bottling must be coordinated with brewing, and this can be difficult in a one-person operation. Cast-out wort should be cooled to at least 86 degrees F (30 degrees C) before it is mixed in with the young beer. Microbrewers may want to filter this wort, but it is not necessary. Remember to use wort that is not excessively hopped.

First runnings from the lauter-tun can also be used as Speise extract for the bottle conditioning, but they must be boiled in order to sterilize them. Having to sterilize this form of Speise may be inconvenient for some breweries, but many breweries swear by this practice and insist that the resulting beers are smoother than those that were primed with cast-out wort.

Kraeusen beer can also be used for priming, either from another batch of Weissbier or from a lager fermentation that is in high kraeusen. Using kraeusen from a bottom-fermented beer will help the natural clarification process in the bottle and increase the shelf life of the beer (lager yeast tends to settle out of solution better and is less inclined to autolyze than top-fermenting yeast). These benefits also accrue when lager yeast is added to the young-beer/Speise mixture, but for brewers who are working only with top-fermenting yeast, using lager yeast may be impractical.

The bottling process for Weissbier is relatively simple. Because Weissbier is bottle- or keg-conditioned, counter-pressure filling is not necessary. Oxygen uptake during packaging is not a great concern either, as any oxygen brought into solution can be metabolized by the yeast. However, excessive oxygen uptake should be avoided, lest the beer take on an oxidized character.

To this end, the mixing apparatus for the young beer, Speise and yeast can be designed in a variety of ways to minimize oxygen uptake while still distributing the elements of the mixture thoroughly and evenly in the mixing vessel. For the homebrewer this apparatus can be as simple as a plastic bucket and stainless-steel spoon. Simply stir the wort and yeast into the mixing bucket or pot with the spoon just prior to bottling and, if possible, continue to agitate while siphoning off into the bottles or keg to avoid stratification of the Speise and young beer (wort is denser than beer, so if the mixture is left to stand it may begin to separate). It is important to not rouse or splash the mixture when stirring.

Microbrewers may want to design some type of mixing vessel that will evenly combine the young beer, Speise and yeast, such as a tank with an agitation system or with a pump that circulates the mixture (see pg 76). In-line dosing is another option for commercial brewers, although this method may require greater capital expenditure.

If the young beer has not been filtered, adding yeast to the bottle or the mixture may be superfluous, particularly if the warm conditioning occurs at higher temperatures. Otherwise, add yeast to the mixture to ensure a thorough fermentation in the bottle. A good rule of thumb is to add 1 liter of thick yeast to every hectoliter of Speise. For homebrew recipes this equates to about 10 milliliters, or one-third ounce per quart of Speise used.

A counter-pressure filler is not required for packaging and, since a classically brewed, bottle-conditioned Hefe Weissbier is served with its yeast sediment, brewers who are not equipped with filters or counter-pressure bottlers do not have to be excluded from the ranks of those who make the finest quality Weissbiers. Regardless of the bottling method chosen, excessive oxygen uptake should be avoided, and bottling must take place under conditions of maximum sterility to avoid an infection. Fully attenuated beer is relatively low in available nutrients for any microorganisms present, but the Speise is rich in unfermented extract and assimilable nitrogen compounds, so a trace infection can drastically alter the character of the finished beer. Because Weissbier is conditioned at warm temperatures, such damage will be particularly explicit if undesirable microflora having a higher temperature optimum are present (e.g., *Lactobacillus* or *Pediococcus*).

The traditional conditioning procedures can be carried out quite easily by the homebrewer or microbrewer who packages in kegs or bottles, since these containers are able to withstand the high pressures that result from the bottle or keg conditioning. Conditioning is more difficult for the pubbrewer or the brewer who is making Kristall Weizen; the conditioning tanks must be able to withstand pressures of at least 40 psi, and in many cases somewhat more. This translates to increased expenditure when tanks are being purchased. If the beer is warm conditioned at a cooler temperature (57 degrees F, 14 degrees C), and a lower degree of carbonation is chosen (0.55 percent by weight), then the conditioning tank must be able to withstand pressures of only 30 psi. In any case, the higher degree of carbonation found in Weissbiers will make dispensing from a keg or tank somewhat tricky. Remember, if the beer is to be touted as a true Reinheitsgebot Weissbier, whether it is a Kristall, Hefe or Berliner Weissbier, the carbonation must be natural or come from CO_2 that has been recovered from the fermentations in that brewery.

RECIPE FORMULATION

One problem with attempting to duplicate the taste of a particular German Hefe Weizen has to do with the choice of malt. It is relatively difficult to obtain German malts in the United States so it is usually necessary to compromise by using American or British malts. German malts vary greatly from American malts simply because of the vast difference in climates. German malts are for the most part considered to be maritime, whereas North American barley and wheat is grown mainly in a continental climate. The differences between maritime and continental grains can be great in terms of both content and structure of protein, polyphenol, starch and phenol precursors, all factors which greatly affect the quality and flavor of the beer.

Though they are highly modified, British or other malts produced from maritime barleys will probably emulate German malts better than the high protein malts made from the continental barleys of the United States. Some Canadian malts may also be well suited for brewing a Weissbier. The advantage of using an American malt is that, because of its increased protein content, it has probably been more highly modified and is enzymatically more powerful than a German malt. American malt thus makes infusion mashing more workable for those breweries not equipped for decoction mashing.

Unless otherwise specified, yields of 83 percent for wheat malt and 78 percent for barley malt are assumed, both expressed in air dry substance. A yield difference of 5 percent is assumed for both the 5-gallon and 1-barrel recipes. These figures were chosen based on empirical observations; if they do not reflect the efficiency of your brewing process, adjust accordingly.

It is impractical to specify a particular amount of hops that should be dosed to a brew. To say "1 ounce of Hallertauer hersbrucker" would make accuracy impossible, as it disregards any variation of alpha acid content due to growing region, year, or the form of the hop. Cone or normal pelletized Hallertauer hersbrucker may have an alpha acid content of 3 percent, enriched pellets may have double that concentration, and extracts will contain at least 10 percent. Hop rates are expressed in these recipes in terms of alpha acid content, based on the projected IBU of the beer and assuming an average yield of bittering substances. To calculate the correct amount of hops or hop products to add to the boil, take the given g/bbl or g/5 gallon figure and divide by the alpha content. If the recipe calls for 4 g alpha acid per barrel and the alpha acid content of the specified hop is 5 percent, then 80 g of that hop must be added per barrel of wort. To express in HBU for one barrel, first convert grams of hops to ounces. There are 28 g per ounce, so 80 g = 2.86 ounces.

HBU = ounces of hops used x alpha acid of hops

= 2.86 x 5 percent

= 14.3

All recipe calculations are based on the specified cast out quantity. To convert 5-gallon recipes to 1-barrel recipes, multiply amounts of malt or malt extract, hops, water, yeast and Speise by 6.2.

EXTRACT RECIPES

- Hans' Hefe Weizen -

Original gravity: 1.050 (12.4 °Plato)
Apparent degree of attenuation: 70 percent
IBU: 15

Ingredients for 5 gallons
4 pounds (1.8 kg) pale malt extract
4 pounds (1.8 kg) wheat malt extract
0.75 g alpha acid, using Perle or Hallertauer hops (2.6 HBU)
1 1/2 quarts of Speise for priming
3 7/10 ounces (110 mL) liquid Weissbier yeast

Ingredients for 1 barrel
24 4/5 pounds (11.1 kg) pale malt extract
24 4/5 pounds (11.1 kg) pale wheat extract
4.65 g alpha acid, using Perle or Hallertauer hops (16 HBU)
2 1/3 gallons of Speise for priming
23 ounces (680 mL) liquid Weissbier yeast

Procedures for 5 gallons [1 barrel]
After the water has come to a boil, dissolve the liquid or dry extract by stirring vigorously, being careful not to allow any of the extract to burn on the bottom of the pot. Add half of the hops as soon as the mixture begins to boil, another quarter after half an hour and the last quarter 50 minutes after the boil begins. After one hour remove from heat and

cool to 60 degrees F (15.6 degrees C). Save 1 1/2 quarts [2 1/3 gallons] of wort in an aseptically sealed container and store it in the refrigerator. Having properly aerated the wort, pitch 3.4 ounces (100 mL) [21 ounces (620 mL)] of the Weissbier yeast and allow to ferment at 59 degrees F (15 degrees C) for three to four days or until it is apparent that the beer is fully attenuated. Rack the Weissbier from the glass carboy or other fermentation vessel into a mixing vessel that will hold the entire batch of beer. When approximately half the beer has been racked into this vessel add the Speise and the remainder of the Weissbier yeast. Then add the rest of the beer. Stir thoroughly, making every effort not to splash the beer. Rack into bottles or container, seal and store for five days at room temperature (at least 65 degrees F). Afterward, refrigerate at a temperature of 39 to 47 degrees F (4 to 8 degrees C) for three weeks. Serve at 47 degrees F (8 degrees C), pouring slowly into the glass. Serve with or without Hefe!

- Old Bavarian Dunkles Weissbier -

Original gravity: 1.050 (12.4 °Plato)
Apparent degree of attenuation: 68 percent
IBU: 16

Ingredients for 5 gallons
4 pounds (1.8 kg) dark malt extract
4 pounds (1.8 kg) wheat malt extract
0.8 g alpha acid, using Tettnanger or Hallertauer hops (2.8 HBU)
1 1/2 quarts Speise for priming
3 7/10 ounces (110 mL) liquid Weissbier yeast

Ingredients for 1 barrel
24 4/5 pounds (11.1 kg) dark malt extract
24 4/5 pounds (11.1 kg) wheat malt extract
4.95 g alpha acid, using Tettnanger or Hallertauer hops (17.4 HBU)
2 1/3 gallons Speise for priming
23 ounces (680 mL) liquid Weissbier yeast

Procedures for 5 gallons [1 barrel]
Brew similarly to the pale Weissbier, but with this beer add the second kettle hops after 40 minutes and the aroma hops after 55 minutes. Total boil time should be 70 minutes. Cool the wort to 56 degrees F (13 degrees C) and ferment at 68 degrees F (20 degrees C) for three days or until attenuation appears complete. Rack, prime and package in similar fashion to **Hans' Hefe Weissbier**, but make sure the warm conditioning takes place at 68 to 77 degrees F (20 to 25 degrees C) for five days. Then, cold condition similar to Hans' for four weeks. A wonderfully smooth, malty, fruity and phenolic balance will overwhelm the senses when this beer is poured gently into a glass and drunk at 49 degrees F (9 degrees C).

ALL-GRAIN FORMULATIONS

- Isar Weizen -

This is the classic of classics, the typical Munich area Hefe Weissbier with a grist composition of 70 to 30 wheat to barley. If the proper yeast is used, your beer should be as good as the original.

Original gravity: 1.055 (13.5 °Plato)
Apparent degree of attenuation: 82 percent
IBU: 15

Ingredients for 5 gallons
5 1/8 pounds (2.3 kg) pale wheat malt
2 2/5 pounds (1.1 kg) pale barley malt
0.75 g alpha acid, using Hallertauer hops (2.6 HBU)
1 4/5 quarts Speise if fresh wort is used, or save 1 3/5 quarts
of Speise for priming
3 2/5 ounces (100 mL) liquid Weissbier yeast
1/3 ounce (10 mL) liquid lager yeast

Ingredients for 1 barrel
31 3/5 pounds (14.3 kg) pale wheat malt
14 7/8 pounds (6.8 kg) pale barley malt
4.65 g alpha acid, using Hallertauer hops (16.1 HBU)
2 3/4 gallons Speise if fresh wort is used, or save 2 1/2 gallons
of Speise for priming
21 ounces (620 mL) liquid Weissbier yeast
2 ounces (60 mL) liquid lager yeast

Procedures for 5 gallons [1 barrel]
Mash in 2 7/10 gallons (10.2 L) [16 7/10 gallons (63.2 L)] of
water at 104 degrees F (40 degrees C) and heat in 10 minutes
to 122 degrees F (50 degrees C). Rest at this temperature for
25 minutes and then pull the first decoction, which should
be thick and should constitute roughly 40 percent of the
mash volume. While maintaining the rest mash temperature, heat the decoction in 15 minutes to 160 degrees F (71
degrees C) and pause here for 15 minutes for a saccharification rest. Heat in 15 minutes to boiling and hold for 20
minutes. Mix the two mashes over the course of 10 minutes.
Adjust the temperature to 147 degrees F (64 degrees C) if it is
not already at this temperature. Rest here for 20 minutes
and then heat in seven minutes to the same saccharification
temperature given above or slightly higher. Rest here until
the iodine reaction is negative. Heat to 170 degrees F (77

degrees C) in five minutes, hold there for five minutes, then transfer to the lauter-tun. Lauter slowly and carefully to avoid a set mash. If a set mash does occur, or if the runoff is sluggish, use a knife to cut gently through the mash, being careful not to cut through the false bottom. Boil for two hours. Add half the hops at the start of the boil, another quarter at 60 minutes and the final quarter at 105 minutes. After the boil ends, allow the wort to stand for a half hour before cooling to 59 degrees F (15 degrees C). Pitch top-fermenting Weissbier yeast and ferment at 65 degrees F (18 degrees C) until fully attenuated (48 to 72 hours). Rack the young beer off the sediment into the mixing vessel, add Speise and liquid lager yeast, and mix gently but thoroughly. Fill into bottles or other container and condition warm at 68 degrees F (20 degrees C) for five days. Store cold for three to four weeks before serving at 45 degrees F (7 degrees C) with sediment in a Weissbier glass.

- Reunification Berliner Weisse -

This will be a tricky one, considering a *Lactobacillus* culture is used in conjunction with the yeast, but if all goes well, the finished beer will be one that even a Berliner would be proud of.
Original gravity: 1.032 (8 °Plato)
Apparent degree of attenuation: 90 percent
IBU: 6

Ingredients for 5 gallons
2 1/8 pounds (0.95 kg) pale barley malt
2 1/8 pounds (0.95 kg) pale wheat malt
0.32 g alpha, using Perle hops (1 HBU)
2 3/4 quarts Speise if fresh wort is being used, otherwise save
2 1/3 quarts of wort for priming

4 3/4 ounces (140 mL) top-fermenting German yeast (not Weizen yeast, but Kölsch or alt yeast)
1 ounce (30 mL) *Lactobacillus delbrückii*

Ingredients for 1 barrel
13 pounds (5.9 kg) pale barley malt
13 pounds (5.9 kg) pale wheat malt
2 g alpha acid, using Perle hops (6.2 HBU)
4 1/4 gallons Speise if fresh wort is being used, or save 3 5/8 gallons of wort for priming
29 1/2 ounces (870 mL) top-fermenting German yeast (not Weizen yeast)
6 1/4 ounces (185 mL) *Lactobacillus delbrückii*

Procedures for 5 gallons [1 barrel]
Mash in 2 1/8 gallon (8 L) [13 1/8 gallons (49.6 L)] water at 104 degrees F (40 degrees C) and hold for 10 minutes. Heat in 10 minutes to 122 degrees F (50 degrees C) and hold for 35 minutes. Heat in 10 minutes to 144 degrees F (62 degrees C) and hold for 10 minutes. Heat to 147 degrees F (64 degrees C) and hold for 20 minutes. Heat to saccharification temperature of 162 degrees F (72 degrees C) and hold for 20 minutes or until the iodine test is negative. Heat to 169 degrees F (76 degrees C), hold for 5 minutes, then transfer to lauter-tun. Sparge at 172 degrees F (78 degrees C). Boil the wort for 105 minutes, adding half the hops at the start of the boil and the other half after 90 minutes. Cool to 59 degrees F (15 degrees C), pitch the yeast and lactic acid bacteria, and ferment isothermically for four days or until attenuation appears to have ceased. Rack, prime, mix well and bottle the young beer. Condition at 59 degrees F (15 degrees C) for 3 months (be patient; it will be worth the wait), and allow some bottles to continue maturing for another 12 to 18 months. Serve at 44 degrees F (7 degrees C) in a schooner. If the beer is too tart for your taste add a dash of raspberry syrup.

- Christoph Probst Weizenbock -

Try to brew this one in late September so it will be ready in time for the holiday season. This is the richest (and strongest) of all Weissbiers, and is sure to bring a smile to the faces of all those who are lucky enough to try it.

Original gravity: 1.064 (16 °Plato)
Apparent degree of attenuation: 76 percent
IBU: 15

Ingredients for 5 gallons
3 1/2 pounds (1.6 kg) Munich dark malt
5 1/3 pounds (2.4 kg) wheat malt
0.75 g alpha acid, using Perle hops (2.6 HBU)
1 1/2 quarts Speise if fresh wort is being used, or save 1 1/4 quarts wort for priming
5 ounces (150 mL) Weissbier yeast

Ingredients for 1 barrel
21 3/4 pounds (9.9 kg) Munich dark malt
33 pounds (14.9 kg) wheat malt
4.65 g alpha acid, using Perle hops (16.1 HBU)
2 3/8 gallons Speise if fresh wort is being used, or save 1 7/8 gallons wort for priming
31 ounces (930 mL) Weissbier yeast

Procedures for 5 gallons [1 barrel]
Mash in 3 1/8 gallons (11.7 L) [19 3/8 gallons (74.4 L)] water at 104 degrees F (40 degrees C) and hold for five minutes. Heat to 122 degrees F (50 degrees C) in 10 minutes and hold for 25 minutes. Pull off the thickest 30 to 40 percent of the mash and heat in 15 minutes to 160 degrees F (71 degrees C). Allow to saccharify for 10 to 15 minutes, then heat in 15

minutes to boiling. Hold the boil for 20 minutes, then add the decoction to the main mash over 10 minutes, raising the temperature of the whole mash to 145 degrees F (63 degrees C). Hold for 10 minutes and then pull the second thick decoction, which should amount to a third of the total mash. Raise the temperature in five minutes to 160 degrees F (71 degrees C), hold for 10 minutes, then heat in 15 minutes to boiling. Boil for 20 minutes and then remix the two mashes, raising the temperature of the whole to 147 degrees F (72 degrees C). Allow to saccharify for 15 minutes or until the iodine test is negative. Heat to 169 degrees F (76 degrees C), hold for five to 10 minutes and then transfer to the lauter-tun. Sparge at 170 to 174 degrees F (77 to 79 degrees C) and rake with a knife if necessary. Boil for two hours, adding half of the hops at the start of the boil, another quarter after one hour and the last quarter 10 minutes before the boil's end. Cool to 59 degrees F (15 degrees C), pitch about 4 1/2 ounces (135 mL) [28 ounces (835 mL)] of the yeast and ferment at 63 degrees F (17 degrees C) for four to seven days, or until attenuation has ceased. If possible, cool the young beer to 41 degrees F (5 degrees C) and hold for five days before racking to clarify. Rack, prime, add the remaining yeast, and bottle or keg. Condition warm at 68 degrees F (20 degrees C) for five to seven days, and then store at 39 to 46 degrees F (4 to 8 degrees C) for five weeks. Serve at 47 degrees F (9 degrees C) in a Weissbier glass with sediment.

- Austrian-style Kristall Weizen -

Kristall Weizen is more popular in Austria than Germany, and may be enjoyed at any time of year. Whether you have just climbed the highest mountain or you are taking a break from the skiing at Kitzbühel, this is the style of Weissbier that you'll find at mountain lodges in the Austrian Alps. This form of Weissbier is commonly served with a lemon slice.

Original gravity: 1.050 (12.5 °Plato)
Apparent degree of attenuation: 84 percent
IBU: 12

Ingredients for 5 gallons
3 pounds (1.4 kg) pale barley malt
5 1/8 pounds (2.3 kg) pale wheat malt
0.6 g alpha acid, using Cascade hops (2.1 HBU)
2 3/8 quart Speise if fresh wort is being used, or save 2 quarts wort for priming
3 ounces (90 mL) liquid Weissbier yeast
1/3 ounces (10 mL) liquid lager yeast

Ingredients for 1 barrel
19 pounds (8.6 kg) pale barley malt
32 pounds (14.5 kg) pale wheat malt
3.5 g alpha acid, using Cascade hops (12.7 HBU)
3 7/10 gallons Speise if fresh wort is being used, or save 3 1/8 gallons wort for priming
19 ounces (550 mL) liquid Weissbier yeast
2 ounces (60 mL) liquid lager yeast

Procedures for 5 gallons [1 barrel]
Mash in 3 1/8 gallons (11.7 L) [19 1/8 gallons (72.4 L)] water at 104 degrees F (40 degrees C) and raise the temperature of the mash 1 degree C per minute to 122 degrees F (50 degrees C). Rest at this temperature for 40 minutes, then raise the temperature of the mash to 147 degrees F (64 degrees C) in 15 minutes. Rest for 10 minutes and pull a thick decoction that constitutes roughly 40 percent of the mash. Heat the

decoction to 161 degrees F (72 degrees C) in five minutes and hold for 10 to 15 minutes, or until saccharification is complete. Heat in 15 minutes to boiling and hold for 15 minutes. Remix the mashes slowly, raising the temperature of the whole to 161 degrees F (72 degrees C). Allow to saccharify, then raise the temperature of the mash to 170 degrees F (77 degrees C). Hold for five minutes and transfer to the lauter-tun. Sparge at 170 to 176 degrees F (77 to 80 degrees C). Boil for two hours adding half of the hops at the start of the boil, another quarter after 60 minutes and the last quarter after 105 minutes. Remove hot trub and, if possible, cold trub as well. Cool the wort to 59 degrees F (15 degrees C) and pitch the Weissbier yeast. Ferment isothermically at 63 degrees F (17 degrees C) until attenuation has ceased. Rack to a settling tank. The temperature of the beer should be approximately 41 degrees F (5 degrees C). Allow to settle for five to seven days and rack into a tank or other vessel into which the Speise and lager yeast have been placed. Allow to condition at 45 degrees F (7 degrees C) for two weeks, setting the bunging pressure at approximately 28 psi or 2 bar. Microbrewers should filter the beer prior to kegging or bottling, and if the shelf life of the beer is supposed to be longer than two months, undertake some means of protein/polyphenol stabilization to increase the chemical-physical stability of the beer. Serve with or without a lemon slice at 46 degrees F (8 degrees C).

Note: If decoction mashing is not a possibility, then use well modified malts and mash isothermically at 149 to 151 degrees F (65 to 66 degrees C) for 80 minutes.

- Old Bavarian Weissbier -

The color of this ruddy brew conjures up images of a full-bodied beer that is best enjoyed with a hearty meat-and-potatoes meal. This beer most likely resembles many of the earlier Weissbiers in color, as the earlier malts were not as pale as those today. Enjoy any time of day, in any season.

Original gravity: 1.055 (13.5 °Plato)
Apparent degree of attenuation: 80 percent
IBU: 12

Ingredients for 5 gallons
2 1/8 pounds (0.95 kg) Munich dark malt
4 5/8 pounds (2.2 kg) pale wheat malt
3/16 pound (.07 kg) dextrin malt (crystal or cara dark)
0.6 g alpha acid, using Perle or Hallertauer hops (2.1 HBU)
2 1/4 quarts Speise if fresh wort is being used, or save 1 7/8 quarts wort for priming
2 3/4 ounces (80 mL) liquid Weissbier yeast
1/3 ounce (10 mL) liquid lager yeast

Ingredients for 1 barrel
13 pounds (6 kg) Munich dark malt
29 pounds (13.2 kg) pale wheat malt
1 pound (0.45 kg) dextrin malt (crystal or cara dark)
3.5 g alpha acid, using Perle or Hallertauer hops (12.7 HBU)
3 3/5 gallons (11.5 L) Speise
17 ounces (500 mL) Weissbier yeast
2 ounces (60 mL) lager yeast

Procedures for 5 gallons [1 barrel]
Mash in 2 3/8 gallons (9.2 L) [15 gallons (57 L)] water at 104 degrees F (40 degrees C) and raise the mash temperature in 15 minutes to 122 degrees F (50 degrees C). Hold a protein rest for 30 minutes and then pull a thick decoction that amounts to 30 to 40 percent of the total mash. Heat the decoction in 10 to 15 minutes to 147 degrees F (64 degrees C) and hold here for 10 minutes. Heat in 10 minutes to 158

degrees F (70 degrees C), hold for 15 minutes and then bring to a boil. Boil for 30 minutes and then recombine the mashes slowly, raising the temperature of the whole to 147 degrees F (64 degrees C). Rest at this temperature for 10 to 15 minutes and then heat to the saccharification temperature of 161 degrees F (71 degrees C). Allow to saccharify for 15 to 20 minutes, or until conversion has been verified with the iodine test. Heat to 169 degrees F (76 degrees C), hold for five minutes and then transfer to the lauter-tun. Sparge at 176 degrees F (80 degrees C). Boil for two hours, adding half of the hops at the start of the boil, the next quarter after 60 minutes and the last quarter after 105 minutes. Remove the hot trub and cool to 55 degrees F (13 degrees C). Ferment at 68 degrees F (20 degrees C) until fully attenuated. Rack into a settling tank for three to five days, filter, then rack into a mixing tank along with the Speise and bottom-fermenting yeast. Be sure that the contents of the mixing tank are thoroughly mixed before bottling or kegging. Breweries serving directly from a tank should keep the beer at 45 to 50 degrees F (7 to 10 degrees C) and set the bunging pressure at 25 psi or 1.8 bar. Allow to condition for three to four weeks. If bottling or kegging, keep the packaged beer at 68 degrees F (20 degrees C) for five days and then cool the kegs or bottles to 41 to 45 degrees F (5 to 7 degrees C) and store at this temperature for two to three weeks before serving. Enjoy at 48 to 50 degrees F (9 to 10 degrees C).

Appendix 1

SOME CLASSIC WEISSBIER BREWERIES AND THE BEERS THAT MADE THEM FAMOUS

There are almost 200 breweries in Germany alone that produce Weissbier, and it is impossible to list all of them in this book. I have chosen breweries both large and small. Some are well known, while others are located in some of the most obscure regions in Bavaria and sell their beer only in the pub adjacent the brewery. I must confess that I have not tried all of the available Weissbiers, and I am listing only the breweries whose beers I have tried. The more experienced Weissbier drinker may contend that I have omitted certain breweries worthy of distinction, and to this I have only one response: travel to Germany and visit as many Weissbier breweries as possible, using this appendix as a suggestion, but not necessarily a guide.

Brauerei Aying
Franz Inselkammer KG
Zornedinger Str. 1
8011 Aying

Bavaria, Germany
Tel: (08095) 8 80

Located in a village on the outskirts of Munich, the Aying brewery produces a variety of products including four Weissbiers: a Hefe Weissbier, an Export Weissbier, a Dunkles Weissbier and a Weizenbock. The Hefe Weissbier is available in the United States.

Erdinger Weissbräu
Franz Brombach
Lange Zeile 1,3 u. 6
8058 Erding
Bavaria, Germany

Franz Brombach bought the Erdinger Weissbräu in 1935, when it had a yearly capacity of 3,500 hL. Slowly production increased to 100,000 hL by 1970. Then one of the most amazing growth rates ever for a German brewery began, and today in 1991 Erdinger produces more than three-quarters of a million hL per year. The success story is not entirely attributable to high powered marketing techniques; rather, the taste of Erdinger Weissbier is on the neutral side, making it more drinkable to the Weissbier consumer who does not like to be overwhelmed by esters or phenols. Erdinger Weissbier is about as classic a Weissbier as can be found: starting gravity is around 1.049 (12.3 °Plato), color is 5.1 SRM units (12.3 EBC units), CO_2 content is about 4.1 volumes (8 g/L), limit of fermentation is 80 percent,[98] and it is bottle conditioned with a lager yeast. The brewery also produces a Dunkles Weissbier and a Weizenbock called Pikantus. Riding the trendy wave of alcohol-free beers, Erdinger has recently begun selling its own version of an alcohol-free Weissbier, Preminger. Loyalists and purists can only shake their heads and ask, "What *is* the world coming to?"

Weissbräu Freilassing
Bräuhausstr. 5
8228 Freilassing
Bavaria, Germany

This small German brewpub is located in the town of Freilassing, just across the border from Salzburg, Austria. The brewery is about as romantic as they come, complete with a wood-fired copper brewing vessel and open vat fermenters. The brewery makes only Weissbier and, at Christmas time, a Weizenbock.

Gräflich von Moy'sches
Hofbrauhaus Freising, GmbH
Mainburger Str. 26
8050 Freising
Bavaria, Germany

What is arguably one of the best Weissbiers in the world has only been produced by "Moy" since 1976. The Weissbierbrauerei Huber was sold to Moy in the late '70s, but the beer produced is the same as it ever was. Huber Weisses is an institution in Freising, the city that is home to the brewing university and brewery of Weihenstephan. Ironically, all of the students at Weihenstephan indulge themselves not in the Weihenstephaner Weissbier, but in "Huber." The polar bear on the labels, glasses and coasters of this classic Weissbier symbolize quality and tradition in Freising. In fact, when Moy decided to make the Huber Weisses labels more glitzy and put the polar bear in the backround of the label, there was an uproar among the loyal Huber drinkers. Nonetheless, there has been no open boycott of the beer, and one sip of it will tell you why. For

The old Huber Weisses logo...   and the new.

starters, it is one of the least gassy of all Weissbiers, with just 6 g/L of CO_2.[99] Its slightly higher than normal concentration of iso amyl acetate gives it a delightfully fruity nose and flavor. It is a mild tasting Weissbier that is totally top fermented. Moy also produces five other Weissbiers, including a light, a Kristall and a Weizenbock, but Huber accounts for more than 30 percent of Moy's Weissbier sales. Unfortunately none of the Moy products are currently available in North America, but to be able to drink a Huber Weisses in the old Brästüberl of the Weissbierbrauerei Huber is worth the plane fare to Germany.

Bayerische Staatsbrauerei Weihenstephan
8050 Freising-Weihenstephan
Germany
(08161) 3021

Home of the famous German brewing school, Weihenstephan has several breweries. The Weissbier is made in part at the experimental and educational brewery on the campus. The Weihenstephan brewery is purported to be the oldest site for modern brewing in the world. The Hefe Weissbier is very carbonated (almost 9 g/L CO_2)[100] and quite turbid. It is robust and full of flavor. Other wheat beers from Weihenstephan include a Dunkelweizen, a Kristall Weizen and a Leichtes Weissbier.

Schlossbrauerei Kaltenberg
Irmingard prizessin v. Bay. GmbH
Augsburger Str. 41
8080 Fürstenfeldbruck
Bavaria, Germany
(08141) 2430

A so-called "castle brewery," Kaltenberg is famous not only for its beer, but for the "Knight Games" that take place at the castle every summer. This brewery is known more for its dark Weissbier than its paler counterpart, and indeed, the former is an excellent representation of the style.

Weissbierbrauerei Haag
Alois Unertl
Lerchenberger Str. 6
8092 Haag
Bavaria, Germany
(08072) 8297

Unertl Weissbier enjoys almost a cult following in Munich and surroundings, and those who drink Unertl swear by it. The town of Haag lies east of Munich in the heart of wheat beer brewing country. This Weissbier sets itself apart from the mainstream Weissbiers by its appearance alone. It has a beautiful reddish-orange color. This beer overwhelms the taste buds with its bold, complex taste. It is very spicy, and its slightly acidic character makes it very thirst-quenching. Like the Huber Weisses, this is a beer worth seeking out.

Brauerei Hutthurm

Marktplatz 5
8391 Hutthurm
Bavaria, Germany
(08505) 8 44

One of the finest Dunkles Weissbiers I have ever drunk is that of the Hutthurm brewery. A pronounced malty nose is followed up by a deep mouthfeel and an extremely rich, smooth finish.

Brauerei G. Schneider & Sohn KG

Emil-Ott-Str. 5
8420 Kelheim
Bavaria, Germany
(09441) 7050

In the last century, as Weissbier appeared doomed to extinction, Georg Schneider started the Schneider brewery in Munich and in so doing helped to revive the Weissbier style (see Chapter 1). The first Georg Schneider of brewing repute was a pioneer who took a big gamble on his newly acquired brewery and his risky concept. The Dr. Georg Schneider of today, who represents the fifth generation of this prolific brewing family, is at the helm of a brewery that produces several hundred thousand hectoliters of Weissbier and nothing else. The forerunner of the Schneider line of products is the "Schneider Weisse," a rich, full bodied Weissbier. It is not really a pale Weissbier, but it is not dark enough to be a Dunkles Weissbier either; its color of 24 EBC units[101] puts it somewhere in between. The amber color comes in part from the beer's high starting gravity of 1.056 (13.8 °Plato). The high starting gravity also translates to a higher-than-average alcohol content of around 4.5 percent by weight. The bouquet of this beer is both estery and phenolic, and the level of iso amyl acetate is about 4.7 mg/L,[102]

giving the beer a pronounced fruity (banana) aroma. This is a fine example of the style, as double digit growth rates for the product attest.

The Schneider and Sons Brewery is also known for its Weizenbock Aventinus. This rich, creamy beer is actually of doppel bock strength, weighing in at a hefty 1.076 (18.5 °Plato). The alcohol content is also nothing to scoff at: 6.2 percent by weight. Aventinus is a dark Weizen bock, with a color of 120 EBC units.[103] This is a highly attenuated beer (around 80 percent),[104] but it is nonetheless sweet in character.

Though he has clung proudly to his family's long brewing tradition, Schneider has succumbed to the market forces in Germany and now produces a Leichtes Weissbier, "Thal Nr. 10." With only 220 kcal/L and an alcohol content of 1.5 percent by volume, this beer is ideal for the diet-conscious German. I'm not dieting yet, so I prefer the Schneider Weisse and the Aventinus. The future looks bright for Schneider, particularly now that Georg Schneider the Sixth is studying brewing science in Weihenstephan. I would not be surprised to see this beer being marketed in North America in the near future.

Weissbräu Kösslarn
Marktplatz 23
8399 Kösslarn
Bavaria, Germany
(08536) 2 45

This brewery has a special place in my heart, because owner and brewmaster Martin Brunner gave me an in-depth tour of his brewery on short notice, and because he is one of the most interesting brewmasters I have ever met. Having worked in breweries in Africa and the Seychelles, he returned to Germany in his forties to purchase the brewery and adjacent pub in the town of Kösslarn (near the city of Passau). He is a rare example of the dying breed of brewmasters who allow the beer to fully mature and condition before releasing it for sale. This dedication is evident in the quality of his Weissbier, one of Germany's finest.

Brauerei Lorenz Widmann
8015 Markt Schwaben
Bavaria, Germany
(08121) 33 49

Even though I had to wake up at 5:00 a.m. to go toil at

this less-than-modern, human-powered brewery, it is also dear to my heart, because it is where I began my formal training as a brewmaster. Located in the heart of wheat beer brewing country east of Munich, Brauerei Widmann produces as solid an example of Hefe Weissbier as can be

found. The brewery employs classic procedures to make this beer: 70 percent wheat in the grist, single decoction mash, open fermentation at warm temperatures and lager yeast for bottle conditioning. Being a small brewery, the quality of the Widmann Weissbier varies, but, sentimental reasons aside, it is one of the best in the world.

Paulaner-Salvator-Thomas-Bräu AG
Hochstr. 75
8000 München 95
Bavaria, Germany
(089) 41151

Paulaner's Hefe Weissbier is probably the finest of Munich's "Big Six" breweries. Even better, this beer is widely available throughout North America. This beer displays an excellent balance of esters and phenols and, if you smell hard enough, you can detect all of the major flavor components, even a touch of vanilla. Unfortunately, the beer does have a bit of a crackerlike taste that no doubt can be attributed to the fact that it is pasteurized before it is shipped overseas.

**Gabriel Sedylmayr
Spaten-Franziskaner-
Bräu KGaA**
Marsstr. 46-48
8000 München 2
Bavaria, Germany
(089) 51 22 1

Also one of Munich's most popular Weissbiers, the Franziskaner Weissbier accounts for more than 35 percent of Spaten's total beer sales. It is not one of my personal favorites; I find it to be bitterly phenolic and a bit nondescript. But who am I to argue with the beer drinkers in Munich?

Brauerei Hacklberg
Bräuhausplatz 1
8390 Passau
Bavaria, Germany
(0851) 50150

This brewery produces two of the finest Weissbiers I have ever tasted, a light and a dark version that are both called Jakobi. The pale Jakobi is very crisp and refreshing, with a character that is slightly fruity and not overwhelmingly phenolic. It is very pale and has a clean, smooth finish. The Jakobi Dunkles Weissbier is malty, but light and almost tart, with a slight acidic character that makes it very thirst-quenching. Passau is called "the Venice of Germany," but if the beauty of the city is not enough to lure you there, then these two beers will.

Schlossbrauerei Grünbach GmbH
Kellerberg 2
8059 Grünbach
Bavaria, Germany
(08122) 1 21 96

Also located in the heart of wheat beer brewing country to the northeast of Munich, Grünbach produces a variety of Weissbiers, all of which are outstanding. The Benno Scharl Weissbier is full bodied and rich, with an estery note that overshadows the phenolic side of the beer.

Berliner Kindl Brauerei AG
Rollbergstr. 26
1000 Berlin 44
Berlin, Germany
(030) 6 89 92 0

The Kindl brewery is the largest producer of Berliner Weisse in the world, and its product is a fine example of the style. Some criticize the product because it is not bottle conditioned, but it is nonetheless a tasty wheat beer.

Dortmunder Union-Schultheiss Brauerei AG
Methfesselstr. 28-48
1000 Berlin 61
Berlin, Germany
(030) 7 80 03 0

As was described in Chapter 2, the Berliner Weisse from Schultheiss is made in the most painstaking manner. The result is worth the extra effort, as this beer is regarded by most critics as the pinnacle of achievement in the style.

Appendix 2

SOURCES OF YEASTS TO MAKE GERMAN WHEAT BEERS

Hefebank Weihenstephan
8050 Freising
Germany
Tel.: 49 8161 713470
Fax: 49 8161 714181

Versuchs- und Lehranstalt für Brauerei in Berlin
Seestraße 13
1000 Berlin 65
Germany
Tel: 49 30 4 50 91
Fax: 49 30 45 36069

J.E. Siebel Sons' Company Inc.
4055 West Peterson Ave.
Chicago, IL 60646 USA
Tel: (312) 463-3400

Endnotes

1.   F. Erling, 44 Verbrauchergründe für Weißbier-konsum, *Brauwelt* 118:17, April 27, 1978, p. 594.

2.   Gauweiler kritisiert den Vormarsch des Dosenbieres, *Handelsblatt*, February 2, 1991, p. 20.

3.   F. Erling, 44 Verbrauchergründe für Weißbier-konsum, p. 594.

4.   Ibid., p. 597.

5.   *Handbuch der Brauerei-Praxis*, Verlag Hans Carl, Nürnberg, Germany, 1989, p. 94.

6.   Gauweiler kritisiert den Vormarsch des Dosenbieres, *Handelsblatt*, February 2, 1991, p. 20.

7.   L. Narziß, *Die Technologie der Würzebereitung*, Ferdinand Enke Verlag, Stuttgart, Germany, 1985, p. 354.

8.   Ibid., p. 23.

9.   L. Narziß, *Abriß der Bierbrauerei*, Ferdinand Enke Verlag, Stuttgart, Germany, 1986, p. 356.

10.   Ibid., p. 356.

11.   Ibid., p. 356.

12.   Ibid., p. 356.

13.   Ibid., p. 357.

14.   Ibid., p. 357.

15. Ibid., p. 357.
16. H. M. Eßlinger, Herstellung von Leichtbier in der Praxis, *Brauwelt* 131:11, March 14, 1991, p. 381.
17. Ibid., p. 381.
18. M. Jackson, *The New World Guide to Beer*, Running Press Book Publishers, Philadelphia, Pa., USA, 1988, p. 62.
19. L. Narziß, *Abriß der Bierbrauerei*, p. 359.
20. Ibid., p. 360.
21. Ibid., p. 360.
22. Ibid., p. 360.
23. Ibid., p. 360.
24. Ibid., p. 360.
25. Ibid., p. 360.
26. Ibid., p. 360.
27. A. Piendl, 500 Biere aus Aller Welt, Deutsche Untergärige und Obergärige Leichtbiere und Schankbiere, *Brauindustrie* 71:15, August, 1986, pp. 968-969.
28. Ibid., pp. 968-969.
29. Ibid., pp. 968-969.
30. M. Jackson, *The New World Guide to Beer*, p. 63.
31. A. Piendl, 500 Biere aus Aller Welt, Deutsche Untergärige und Obergärige Leichtbiere und Schankbiere, pp. 968-969.
32. L. Narziß, *Abriß der Bierbrauerei*, p. 358.
33. *Brautechnische Analysenmethoden, Band II*, Selbstverlag der MEBAK, Freising, Germany, 1987, p. 80.
34. L. Narziß, *Abriß der Bierbrauerei*, p. 358.
35. L. Narziß, Hefeweißbier, Rohstoffe und Technologie, *Brauwelt* 123:6, February 10, 1983, p. 199.
36. K. Wackerbauer and P. Krämer, Bayerisches Weizenbier-eine Alternative, *Brauwelt* 122:17, April 29, 1982, p. 760.
37. Ibid., p. 758.
38. Ibid., p. 762.

39. Ibid., p. 762.

40. Ibid., p. 762.

41. Kieninger et al, Über die Veränderung wertbestimmender Stoffgruppen bei der Herstellung von bayerischen Weizenbieren, p. 14.

42. Ibid., p. 13.

43. Ibid., p. 13.

44. Ibid., pp. 14-18, 55.

45. Ibid., p. 55.

46. Ibid., p. 55.

47. K. Wackerbauer and P. Krämer, Bayerisches Weizenbier-eine Alternative, p. 762.

48. Ibid., p. 762.

49. Untersuchungen zur Optimierung der Weizenbierqualität, *Brauwelt* 131:32, August 8, 1991, p. 1360.

50. L. Narziß, *Abriß der Bierbrauerei*, p. 209.

51. L. Narziß, Hefeweißbier, Rohstoffe und Technologie, p. 199.

52. G. Schmidt, Rund um das Hefeweizenbier, *Brauwelt* 118:17, April 27, 1978, p. 583.

53. K. Wackerbauer and P. Krämer, Bayerisches Weizenbier-eine Alternative, p. 716.

54. L. Narziß, *Abriß der Bierbrauerei*, p. 347.

55. S. Donhauser, *Technologie der Gärung, Lagerung und Abfüllung*, Lecture notes, Spring 1990.

56. L. Narziß, *Abriß der Bierbrauerei*, p. 347.

57. L. Narziß, Hefeweißbier, Rohstoffe und Technologie, p. 199.

58. Ibid., p. 199.

59. G. Schmidt, Rund um das Hefeweizenbier, p. 583.

60. K. Wackerbauer and P. Krämer, Bayerisches Weizenbier-eine Alternative, p. 716.

61. L. Narziß, *Abriß der Bierbrauerei*, p. 311.

62. A. Piendl, 500 Biere aus Aller Welt, Deutsche

Hefefreie Weizen Vollbiere, *Brauindustrie* 69:21, November, 1984, p. 1719.

63. J. Guinard, *Lambic*, Brewers Publications, Boulder, Colo., USA, 1990, p. 49.

64. A. Piendl, 500 Biere aus Aller Welt, Deutsche Hefehaltige Weizen Vollbiere, *Brauindustrie* 69:7, April, 1984, pp. 484-85.

65. F. Nitzsche, Analysenergebnisse der Weizenbiere des DLG Jahres 1988, excerpt from dissertation, Technologie der Brauerei I, Freising, Germany, 1990.

66. K. Wackerbauer and P. Krämer, Bayerisches Weizenbier-eine Alternative, p. 759.

68. *Handbuch der Brauerei-Praxis*, 1989, p. 66.

68. L. Narziß, *Die Technologie der Malzbereitung*, Ferdinand Enke Verlag, Stuttgart, Germany, 1976, p. 31

69. J. W. Pence. and D. K. Mecham, Recent Advances in Studies on Wheat Proteins, *Wallerstein Lab. Comm.* 25:86, April, 1962, p. 37.

70. L. Narziß, *Die Technologie der Malzbereitung*, p. 14.

71. D. J. Stevens, Aleurone Layer of Wheat, *Journal of Science, Food and Agriculture* 24, 1973, p. 307.

72. L. Narziß, *Die Technologie der Malzbereitung*, p. 342.

73. Ibid., p. 343.

74. Ibid., p. 343.

75. Ibid., p. 343.

76. *Brautechnische Analysenmethoden, Band I*, Selbstverlag der MEBAK, Freising, Germany, 1984, pp. 191, 193, 194, 197, 212, 237.

77. L. Narziß, Hefeweißbier, Rohstoffe und Technologie, p. 198.

78. Ibid., p. 198.

79. Ibid., p. 198.

80. Ibid., p. 198.

81. L. Narziß, *Abriß der Bierbrauerei*, p. 354.

82. H. Kieninger, Malzeinsatz bei Obergärigen Bieren, *Brauwelt* 117:25, June 23, 1977, p. 822.

83. L. Narziß, *Die Technologie der Würzebereitung*, p. 128.

84. L. Narziß and A. Schwill-Miedaner, Untersuchungen von Winterweizen der Ernten 1988 und 1989, *Brauwelt* 131:4, January 24, 1991, p. 109.

85. Ibid., p. 106.

86. *Brauwelt Brevier 1991*, Verlag Hans Carl, Nürnberg, Germany, 1991, p. 107.

87. L. Narziß, Hefeweißbier, Rohstoffe und Technologie, p. 198.

88. L. Narziß, *Abriß der Bierbrauerei*, p. 355.

89. 4-Vinylguajakol bei der Weizenbierherstellung, *Brauwelt* 130:27, July 5, 1990, p. 1115.

90. Ibid., p. 1115.

91. Ibid., p. 1115.

92. Ibid., p. 1115.

93. Ibid., p. 1115.

94. K. Wackerbauer and P. Krämer, Bayerisches Weizenbier-eine Alternative, p. 762.

95. H. Kieninger, Das Bayerische Weizenbier, *Brauwelt* 118:49, December 7, 1978, p. 1896.

96. L. Narziß, Hefeweißbier, Rohstoffe und Technologie, p. 199.

97. L. Narziß, *Die Technologie der Würzebereitung*, pp. 127-129.

98. A. Piendl, 500 Biere aus Aller Welt, Deutsche Hefehaltige Weizen Vollbiere, *Brauindustrie* 69:7, April, 1984, pp. 484-85.

99. Ibid., pp. 484-485.

100. Ibid., pp. 484-485.

101. Ibid., pp. 484-485.

102. Ibid., pp. 484-485.

103. A. Piendl, 500 Biere aus Aller Welt, Deutsche Untergärige und Obergärige Doppelbockbiere, *Brauindustrie* 70:1, January, 1985, p. 61.

104. Ibid., p. 61.

Glossary

alcohol by volume. A measurement of the alcohol content of a solution in terms of the percentage volume of alcohol per volume of beer. To approximately calculate (margin of error ± 15 percent) the volumetric alcohol content, subtract the final gravity from the original gravity and divide the result by 7.5. For example: 1050-1082 = 38/7.5 = 5% v/v.

alcohol by weight. A measurement of the alcohol content of a solution in terms of the percentage weight of alcohol per volume of beer. Example: 3.2 percent alcohol by weight = 3.2 grams of alcohol per 100 centiliters of beer. The percent of alcohol by weight figure is approximately 20 percent lower than the "by volume" figure because alcohol weighs less than its equivalent volume of water.

aleurone layer. The layer of large, thick-walled cells at the edge of the endosperm in barley, wheat and other cereal grains. Composed of protein and fat, these cells form a triple layer in barley and a single layer in wheat.

Altbier. A traditional style of beer brewed mainly in Düsseldorf but also in Münster, Korschenbroich, Krefeld, Issum and a few other cities of Northern Rhineland and Westphalia. The German word alt means old or ancient and refers to the fact that these beers are brewed by the traditional method of top fermentation that predated the relatively new method of bottom fermentation. Alt beers have a deep, luminous, copper color. They are brewed from dark malts, are well hopped and have a slightly fruity, bittersweet flavor. Their alcohol content varies from 3.5 to 4.0 percent by weight (4.4 to 5.0 percent by volume) and are brewed from an original gravity of about 12.5 °Balling.

amino acid. Any of the organic acids whose molecules contain one or more acidic carboxyl groups (COOH) and one or more amino groups (NH2) and that polymerize to form peptides and proteins. During the beermaking process, amino acids are formed by the enzymatic degradation of proteins. During kilning, amino acids combine with simple sugars to form colored compounds called melanoidins. The critical issue associated with amino acids is their rate of uptake by yeast and the role they play in metabolism. Some amino acids are not essential because yeast can produce their carbon skeletons during metabolism. Others are essential in the sense that they can come only from malt. All amino acids are used by yeast, as nutrients, at different parts of the fermentation.

anthocyanogenes. Phenolic compounds that, depending on their degree of condensation or polymerisation, influence the colloidal stability of beer.

apparent degree of attenuation. The attenuation of beer containing alcohol but no carbon dioxide. It is apparent because it does not represent the extract lost during fermentation, since the drop in gravity caused by the transformation of sugars is added to that of alcohol, which is lighter than water. Apparent attenuation can be converted to real attenuation by multiplying it by 0.819. Since it is easier to measure than real attenuation, it is the method commonly used by brewers, and the term attenuation without qualification invariably means apparent attenuation.

Formula: $A = (B - b)/B \times 100$

A = apparent attenuation in %

B = original gravity in °B (or Plato)

b = gravity of beer devoid of CO_2

attenuation. The percentage reduction in the wort's specific gravity caused by the transformation of contained sugars into alcohol and carbon dioxide gas through fermentation. The fermentable sugars in the wort (which have a higher specific gravity than water) are converted into alcohol (which has a lower specific gravity than water) and carbon dioxide gas (which escapes as gas).

Biersteuergesetz. The German beer tax law, which governs not only the taxation of beer in Germany, but the methods and processes of malting and brewing.

carbonation. The process of injecting or dissolving carbon dioxide gas in a liquid to create an effervescence of pleasant taste and texture. In beermaking, one of three methods is used: 1. injecting the finished beer with the carbon dioxide collected for this purpose during primary fermentation; 2. kraeusening, or adding young fermenting beer to finished beer to induce a renewed fermentation; 3. especially in homebrewing, priming (adding sugar) to fermented wort prior to bottling or to each bottle prior to capping to create a secondary fermentation within the bottle. Fermentation in a sealed bottle or container creates carbon dioxide gas, which, being trapped, dissolves in the beer. The adjective carbonated usually refers to beers artificially injected with carbon dioxide; when caused by priming, the expression bottle-conditioned is more common. Beers intended to be consumed at low temperatures are usually highly carbonated to compensate for the low temperature and vice versa for beers to be drunk at high temperatures. Bottled beer is always carbonated; U.S. draft beers are usually carbonated, while British draft ales are for the most part cask-conditioned.

cast-out wort. Hot wort as it is being cast out from the brew kettle after the boiling process has been completed.

chill haze. Haziness caused by a combination and precipitation of protein matter and tannin molecules during the secondary process of fermentation. It becomes visible when beer is refrigerated too fast, too cold or too long and soon disappears once the beer warms up. It appears around 0 degrees C (32 degrees F) and disappears around 20 degrees C (68 degrees F). It should not be confused with condensation, which is a film of water forming on the exterior of the glass when the glass and beer are cold and the ambient air is warm and moist.

cold trub. The precipitation of protein and tannin material to a fine coagulum during the cooling stage. It starts around 60 degrees C (140 degrees F) and increases as the temperature drops.

cold trub flotation. The process of removing cold trub from cooled wort by subjecting it to an excessive amount of air. Cold trub particles accumulate on the surface of the air bubbles as they rise from the bottom to the top of the flotation vessel, building a layer of foam at the surface of the wort. The wort is then drained from the bottom of the vessel, leaving behind the foam layer and, with it, the cold trub particles. The process may take place in pitched or unpitched wort.

colored beer. Beer with a color of up to 3,000 SRM units (8,000 EBC units) that is added to wort or beer for color adjustment. It is made using a grist composition of roughly three-fifths pale malt and two-fifths color or black malt.

degrees Plato. Plato is a saccharometer expressing the specific gravity as the weight of extract in a 100-gram solution at a temperature of 17.5 degrees C (64 degrees F). This percentage is called degree Plato. The original saccharometer was devised by Balling in 1843 but his tables were slightly erroneous and were later corrected by Dr. Plato for the German Imperial Commission.

DMS. Abbreviation for dimethyl sulfide, a major sulfur compound of lagers not found in British ales because their malts are highly modified at very high temperatures. DMS is released during boiling as a gas that dissipates into the atmosphere. The precursor of DMS, S-methylmethionine, remains present in the wort and converts to DMS if the wort is not cooled rapidly enough (in less than 45 minutes in homebrewing) or if it is allowed to sit after cooling.

EBC. Acronym for European Brewery Convention.

EBC units. Units of measurement for various brewing chemical analyses such as color or bitterness.

esters. Volatile flavor compounds that form through the interaction of organic acids with alcohols during fermentation and contribute to the fruity aroma and flavor of beer.

Exportbier. Tax law subcategory of Vollbier. An Exportbier has a starting gravity of no less than 1.050 (12.5 °Plato) and no more than 1.056 (14 °Plato).

FAN or free amino nitrogen. Generally used to characterize the amount of amino acids in the wort. The FAN content is measured and expressed in parts per million (ppm). A wort of 10 °Balling (1.040) contains approximately 220 ppm of FAN, which is ideal for yeast growth. Raw unmalted barley makes an insignificant contribution to the FAN content.

fatty acids. A group of saturated and unsaturated monobasic aliphatic carboxylic acids, all of which impart a foul, soapy flavor to beer, contribute to its staling and affect its head retention.

first runnings. The first batch of wort removed from the lauter-tun or other straining vessel prior to sparging. It is richer in extract than the wort that follows.

flocculation. The phenomenon by which yeast cells aggregate into masses toward the end of the fermentation process. At the break, top- and bottom-fermenting yeast cells can agglomerate and sink to the bottom, thus contributing to the clarification of the beer. The ability of a yeast (either top or bottom) to flocculate or sediment varies with the strain of yeast.

flotation. *See* cold trub flotation.

fusel alcohols. *See* higher alcohols.

gushing. Phenomenon of a beer foaming vigorously out of the bottle when uncapped. *Syn.* wild beer.

higher alcohols. Alcohols of higher boiling point than ethanol, which are derived from keto-acids during the yeast protein synthesis. The formation of higher alcohols varies with yeast strain and yeast growth, fermentation temperature (an increase in temperature is followed by an increase in the formation of alcohols), and fermentation method (in some cases a stirred fermentation produces more alcohols). There are two classes of higher (fusel) alcohols: volatile alcohols, most often called aliphatic alcohols, and non-volatile alcohols.

hot trub. The coagulation and precipitation of protein matter during the boiling stage. In homebrewing, hot break trub can be improved by the addition of Irish moss during the last 15 minutes of the boil or it can be removed with a hop-back filtration of the wort or by allowing the hot wort to settle out before drawing it to the wort chiller.

IBU. Abbreviation for International Bitterness Unit. An international system of units for measuring and expressing the bitterness in beer based on the parts per million content (or milligrams per liter) of alpha acids.

Note: this formula is an approximation that can be off by as much as 20 percent, depending on hop utilization in the kettle and isoalpha acid loss during fermentation and aging.

Formula: $HBU = H \times (a\% + b\% / 9) / 0.3$

H   = weight of hops in grams per liter (H g/L)

a% = alpha acid percent

b% = beta acid percent

9   = a constant. The flavoring power of alpha acids is about nine times greater than that of beta acids.

0.3 = a constant that represents an approximate 30 percent efficiency rate in hop extraction caused by vaporization or precipitation (boiling, skimming, racking and fining).

Conversely, to calculate the amount of hops in grams per liter required to obtain a specific bitterness unit, the formula is rearranged:

$$H \text{ g/L} = (IBU) / (a\% + b\% / 9) \times 0.3$$

Kjeldahl method. An analytical method of determining the nitrogen content of an organic compound. Named after Johan Kjeldahl.

Kölsch. A very pale, golden-hued, top-fermented beer produced in the metropolitan area of Bonn-Cologne. Under German law, when it is brewed elsewhere in Germany, the name of the locality must precede the word Kölsch. It is highly hopped, mildly alcoholic (±3.7% w/v, 4/6% v/v) and slighly lactic in taste.

kraeusen. The "rocky" or "cauliflower" heads of foam that appear on the surface of the wort during the first days of fermentation. When they reach their peak, between the fourth and seventh day, they are called high kraeusen or rocky heads.

kraeusen beer. Beer that is in the kraeusen stage of fermentation. May be used to kraeusen another batch of beer in a later stage of fermentation to carbonate and condition that beer. *See also* kraeusening.

kraeusening. A method of conditioning that adds a small quantity of young fermenting wort (about 15 to 20 percent) to a fully fermented lagering one to create a secondary fermentation and natural carbonation.

lambic. A unique Belgian wheat beer produced only in a 15-kilometer radius southwest of Brussels in the area called Pajottenland. Lambic is traditionally brewed in winter (October 15 to May 15) because, at that time, a microflora develops in the atmosphere of the Senne River valley, and because the first few months of fermentation must not be too vigorous. The mash, consisting of 60 to 70 percent barley and 30 to 40 percent wheat, is spontaneously fermented by these airborne wild yeasts (*Brettanomyces bruxellensis* and *Brettanomyces cambicus*) and bacteria (thermo bacteria and lactic bacteria). The fermentation vessels consist of large oak or chestnut tuns of 252 gallons each. Fermentation starts after three days. An attentuation of 80 percent is reached after the first summer and is almost complete after the second. Lambic is flavored with old hops, because it must not be bitter, at a rate of 600 grams per hectoliter. Lambic may be served young (three months to one year) or old (at least two years old, usually three to four). Young lambic is very sour, slightly cloudy and produces little or no froth. Old lambic has lost some of its sourness, acquired a vinous bittersweet flavor and produces a fine froth. When young and old lambic are blended, bottled and aged one more year, the end product is called gueuze. In 1965 the terms lambic, gueuze and gueuze-lambic were defined by royal decree: such beers must be made by spontaneous fermentation of a wort of at least 5° Belgian (with a maximum tolerance of 5 percent) containing at least 30 percent wheat, and the packaging must bear the name of the producer and that of the place of origin.

Lactobacillus. Genus name for member of the lactic acid bacteria group. Depending on the particular strain (species), *Lactobacillus* is either homofermentive, producing almost only pure lactate, or heterofermentive, producing other metabolic products in addition to lactate.

Lactobacillus delbrückii. Homofermentive strain (species) of *Lactobacillus* isolated by Professor Max Delbrück. Used in the production of Berliner Weisse.

lautering. The process of separating the spent grains from the sweet wort with a straining apparatus.

lauter-tun. A large vessel fitted with a false slotted bottom and a drain spigot in which the mash is allowed to settle and the sweet wort is removed from the grains through a straining process. In smaller breweries and in the infusion system the mash-tun is used for both mashing and lautering.

modification. 1. The physical and chemical changes occurring in barley during malting. Physically, the grain is rendered millable. Chemically, complex molecules are broken down to simpler, soluble ones by the formation of hydrolytic enzymes which later begin to catalyze the hydrolytic degradation of the starchy endosperm and its cell walls. 2. The degree to which malt has been converted during the malting process as determined by the growth of the acrospire.

modified. Term said of malt to describe the extent of the modification process. American malts are usually undermodified while European, especially English, malts are fully modified.

pH. Abbreviation for potential hydrogen, used to express the degree of acidity and alkalinity in an aqueous solution, usually on a scale of 1 to 14, where H^+ is the hydrogen-ion concentration. Technically, pH is defined as the negative logarithm of the effective hydrogen-ion concentration in gram equivalents per liter of solution: $pH = \log_{10} (1/(H^+))$. A pH value of 7 (pure water at 25 degrees C) indicates neutrality, below 7 (7 to 1) indicates acidity and above 7 (7 to 14) indicates alkalinity. The pH can be measured by specially prepared pH test papers.

phenolic. Usually describes an unpleasant solventlike, medicinal or chemical flavor, but also describes the character of wheat beers made in Southern Germany. The phenolic character of these beers is often described as spicy, or clove-, nutmeg- or vanillalike.

Plato. *See* degrees Plato.

phenols. Volatiles found in small quantities in beer. Higher concentrations, due to the brewing water, infection of the wort by bacteria or wild yeasts, cleaning agents or crown and can linings, impart off-flavors described as phenolic, medicinal or pharmaceutical. Sixty volatile phenolic compounds are present in beer. Their concentration is greater in dark beers than in pale beers.

polyphenol. A complex organic compound partly responsible for chill haze in beer.

protein coagulation. When solutions of water-soluble proteins are heated, the protein becomes denatured at a particular temperature; it then becomes insoluble and either remains in suspension or is precipitated as a clot or curd. Protein coagulation occurs during the wort boiling process and is desirable. It helps remove higher-molecular-weight proteins that can lead to chill haze in the finished beer. The coagulation should not be too complete, however, because higher-molecular-weight proteins also contribute to the body of the beer.

Reinheitsgebot. Initially meaning the Bavarian purity law, the term is now commonly used to mean the German purity law. The original decree was signed in 1516 by Duke Wilhelm IV and it specified that only barley, hops and water could be used to brew beer (yeast was excluded from this ingredient list because at that time brewers were unaware that it was yeast that was fermenting the beer).

saccharification. The process through which starch is converted to sugars and polysaccharides. In the brewing process starch is broken down enzymatically by alpha and beta amylase.

Schankbier. "Light beer." This is a category defined in the German beer tax law which specifies a starting gravity of 1.028 to 1.032 (7 to 8 °Plato). Beers in this category include Leichtes Weissbier and Berliner Weisse.

set mash. A condition that occurs during lautering when the wort is drained too quickly and the bed (fine powder mixed with grain husks) collapses and packs into a tight mass, preventing the flow of the wort.

Speise. A German word that literally means food. This term refers to the wort or other priming sugar that is used to carbonate a top-fermented beer.

SRM (Standard Reference Method) and (European Brewery Convention). Two different analytical methods of describing color developed by comparing color samples. Degrees SRM, approximately equivalent to degrees Lovibond, are used by the ASBC (American Society of Brewing Chemists) while degrees EBC are European units. The following equations show approximate conversions:

$$(°EBC) = 2.65 \times (°Lovibond) - 1.2$$

$$(°Lovibond) = 0.377 \times (EBC) + 0.45$$

Starkbier. In Germany, one of the three legal categories for beers, comprising those brewed from an original gravity of at least 16 °Balling and containing no less than 5 percent alcohol by weight.

TNBS method. Chemical analysis used to determine the content of low-molecular-weight protein compounds in wort or beer.

4-vinyl guaiacol. Phenolic compound usually present in levels above threshold in Southern German style wheat beer. It has a clovelike aroma.

viscosity. The property of a fluid that enables it to resist flowing when it is subject to shear stress. If wort or mash viscosity is too high, then the lautering process may be dramatically impeded. Mash or wort viscosity is usually most greatly influenced by the level of beta glucanes in the malt, as they are extremely viscous.

Vollbier. One of the three legal categories for beers in Germany, comprising those of medium strength brewed from an original gravity of 11 to 14 °Balling and containing 3.5 to 4.5 percent alcohol by weight.

withering. Blowing dry air into barley after germination is complete to decrease the ratio of humidity in the green malt.

yield of extract. The percentage of extractable dry matter in the grist; i.e., the total amount of dry matter that passes into solution in the wort during mashing.

yield. *See* yield of extract.

yield difference. Difference in yield of extract in the laboratory and in a brewery for a given malt. Extract values are determined in a laboratory and are regarded as the greatest possible yield, because the sample grist is very fine and the rest at saccharification temperature is long. Brewery grist is coarser and saccharification rests are shorter, so the extract yield of a malt in a brewery is less than it is in the lab. Modern breweries are able to realize a yield difference that is within 1 percent of the lab value; e.g., if the lab extract value is 80 percent dry weight, the brewery should have a yield that is 79 percent or slightly above.

Index

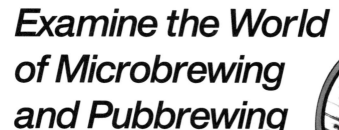

HOMEBREWER?

Get The Whole Story!

Join the thousands of American Homebrewers Association members who read **zymurgy** — the magazine for homebrewers and beer lovers.

Every issue of **zymurgy** is full of tips, techniques, new recipes, new products, equipment and ingredient reviews, beer news, technical articles — the whole world of homebrewing. PLUS, the AHA brings members the National Homebrewers Conference, the National Homebrew Competition, the Beer Judge Certification Program, the Homebrew Club Network, periodic discounts on books from Brewers Publications and much much more.

Mail this coupon today and join the AHA or call now for credit card orders, (303) 447-0816.

BOOKS for Brewers and Beer Lovers

Order Now ... Your Brew Will Thank You!

These books offered by Brewers Publications are some of the most sought after reference tools for homebrewers and professional brewers alike. Filled with tips, techniques, recipes and history, these books will help you expand your brewing horizons. Let the world's foremost brewers help you as you brew. So whatever your brewing level or interest, Brewers Publications has the information necessary for you to brew the best beer in the world — your beer.

- -

Please send me more free information on the following: (check all that apply)

◇ Merchandise & Book Catalog   ◇ Institute for Brewing Studies
◇ American Homebrewers Association   ◇ Great American Beer Festival

Ship to:

Name

Address

City   State/Province

Zip/Postal Code   Country

Daytime Phone   (   )

Payment Method

◇ Check or Money Order Enclosed (Payable to the Association of Brewers)
◇ Visa   ◇ MasterCard

Card Number   Expiration Date

Name on Card   Signature

Brewers Publications, PO Box 1679, Boulder, CO 80306-1679, (303) 447-0816, FAX (303) 447-2825.

BREWERS PUBLICATIONS ORDER FORM

PROFESSIONAL BREWING BOOKS

QTY.	TITLE	STOCK #	PRICE	EXT. PRICE
_____	Brewery Planner	440	80.00	_____
_____	North American Brewers Resource Directory	445	80.00	_____
_____	Principles of Brewing Science	415	29.95	_____

THE BREWERY OPERATIONS SERIES
from Micro and Pubbrewers Conferences

QTY.	TITLE	STOCK #	PRICE	EXT. PRICE
_____	Volume 4, 1987 Conference	424	25.95	_____
_____	Volume 5, 1988 Conference	428	25.95	_____
_____	Volume 6, 1989 Conference	430	25.95	_____
_____	Volume 7, 1990 Conference	433	25.95	_____
_____	Volume 8, 1991 Conference, Brewing Under Adversity	442	25.95	_____
_____	Volume 9, 1992 Conference, Quality Brewing — Share the Experience	447	25.95	_____

CLASSIC BEER STYLE SERIES

QTY.	TITLE	STOCK #	PRICE	EXT. PRICE
_____	Pale Ale	431	11.95	_____
_____	Continental Pilsener	434	11.95	_____
_____	Lambic	437	11.95	_____
_____	Vienna, Märzen, Oktoberfest	444	11.95	_____
_____	Porter	443	11.95	_____
_____	Belgian Ale	446	11.95	_____
_____	German Wheat Beer	448	11.95	_____
_____	Scotch Ale	449	11.95	_____
_____	Bock (available Winter 1993)	452	11.95	_____

BEER AND BREWING SERIES, for homebrewers and beer enthusiasts
from National Homebrewers Conferences

QTY.	TITLE	STOCK #	PRICE	EXT. PRICE
_____	Volume 8, 1988 Conference	427	21.95	_____
_____	Volume 9, 1989 Conference	429	21.95	_____
_____	Volume 10, 1990 Conference	432	21.95	_____
_____	Volume 11, 1991 Conference, Brew Free Or Die!	435	21.95	_____
_____	Volume 12, 1992 Conference, Just Brew It!	436	21.95	_____

GENERAL BEER AND BREWING INFORMATION

QTY.	TITLE	STOCK #	PRICE	EXT. PRICE
_____	Brewing Lager Beer	417	14.95	_____
_____	Brewing Mead	418	11.95	_____
_____	Dictionary of Beer and Brewing	414	19.95	_____
_____	Evaluating Beer	456	25.95	_____
_____	Great American Beer Cookbook	455	24.95	_____
_____	Winners Circle	407	11.95	_____

Call or write for a free *Beer Enthusiast* catalog today.
- U.S. funds only.
- All Brewers Publications books come with a money-back guarantee.
- *Postage & Handling:* $3 for the first book ordered, plus $1 for each book thereafter. Canadian and foreign orders please add $4 for the first book and $2 for each book thereafter. Orders cannot be shipped without appropriate P&H.

SUBTOTAL _____
Colo. Residents Add 3% Sales Tax _____
P & H * _____
TOTAL _____

Brewers Publications, PO Box 1679, Boulder, CO 80306-1679, (303) 447-0816, FAX (303) 447-2825.